Journeys Into John

Journeys Into John

16 Lessons of Exploration and Discovery

Carolyn Thomas, S.C.N., Ph.D.

ST. ANTHONY MESSENGER PRESS
Cincinnati, Ohio

Nihil Obstat: Rev. Edward J. Gratsch
Rev. Thomas Richstatter, O.F.M., S.T.D.

Imprimi Potest: John Bok, O.F.M.

Imprimatur: +Carl K. Moeddel, V.G.
Archdiocese of Cincinnati
April 1, 1998

The *nihil obstat* and *imprimatur* are a declaration that a book is considered to be free from doctrinal or moral error. It is not implied that those who have granted the *nihil obstat* and *imprimatur* agree with the contents, opinions or statements expressed.

Cover and book design by Julie Lonneman
Electronic format and pagination by Sandy L. Digman

ISBN 0-86716-309-7

Published by St. Anthony Messenger Press
Printed in the U.S.A.

Acknowledgments

Without the support and help of many people I could not have completed this work. My special gratitude goes to the managing editor of St. Anthony Messenger Press, Lisa Biedenbach, for inviting me to write this small volume, *Journeys Into John*. I am grateful also to the persons at the Pontifical College Josephinum who assisted me in many ways, especially Msgr. Thomas Olmsted, rector, who encouraged me and stressed the pastoral value of this work for the Church; Peter Veracka, Beverly Lane and the other librarians who assisted me with their expertise; and Beth Kampmeier who provided help with proofreading. To my friends, Sister Julia Head, O.S.U., and Karen Jarboe of the Owensboro, Kentucky, Catholic Center, I owe thanks for assisting in proofreading and offering encouragement. Finally, I am deeply grateful to the Sisters of Charity of Nazareth, my religious congregation, whose inspiration and assistance of many kinds make it possible for me to write.

Dedication

To the faculty and seminarians at the Pontifical College Josephinum and to other students who have challenged me and walked with me on the path of loving insight into the Gospel of John

Contents

Introduction

Journeys Into John, like the first three volumes *(Journeys Into Mark, Journeys Into Matthew* and *Journeys Into Luke)*, is designed for adults who wish to study the Gospel alone or in a group. Rather than simply present-ing factual information, each lesson bears upon human experience, showing how Scripture applies to the lives of Christians who are on their journey with God and to God. The ultimate objective of each journey is to help the reader find in the Gospel of John a means of deepen-ing one's love of Jesus Christ and other people.

Journeys Into John follows the same adult study for-mat of its companion volumes: Exploring (background information), Discovering (reflective exercises), Looking Back (points for review) and Exploring Further (a list of resource materials for further study). The late Raymond Apicella, author of the first three volumes, devised this method of Scripture study.

There are no time limits for any of the journeys since they are designed to accommodate both individual and small-group study. If you are using the book in a group, we encourage you to discuss and share the insights gleaned from each section.

Before You Journey

As we begin this journey into John's Gospel, it is impor-tant to remember that the Gospels emerged from Christian communities of the first century. The Holy Spirit, active in their midst, guided their reflections on the traditions about Jesus' teachings and the meaning of his life, death and resurrection. Each Gospel is unique in many ways: Each evangelist had access to some tradi-tions to which the other authors did not; each evangelist expressed his particular focus on those traditions in his own unique way; each one emphasized different aspects of Jesus' life and teachings in order to respond to the experience, needs and sufferings of a particular Church community.

Most biblical scholars today date the Gospel of John in the last decade of the first century, or at least after the expulsion of the Jewish Christians from the Jewish syna-gogue in 85. That event drove a wedge between Jews who believed that Jesus was the long-awaited messiah of Israel's history and that he was God's Son and those Jews who did not share those beliefs. An anathema was added to the synagogue prayers against any who con-fessed Jesus as the messiah and Son of God, and Jewish

Christians were no longer welcome to participate in syn-agogue worship and activities as they had previously done. That incident brought about the final separation of Jewish Christians from the synagogue and their Jewish counterparts, and it continued to be a source of much contention between them.

Judging from his knowledge of Judaism, we can say that the fourth evangelist appears to have been a Jewish Christian writing for Jewish Christians who had suffered the trauma of this separation. Although ancient tradition identified the authority behind the Fourth Gospel as John, son of Zebedee, one of the Twelve spoken of in the Synoptic Gospels, modern scholars find that the evi-dence does not support this. Rather, the authority behind the Gospel most likely was a companion of Jesus and the "Beloved Disciple" mentioned in the Gospel of John. The author is the one who shaped the Beloved Disciple's traditions about Jesus and the community's reflections on them into the Fourth Gospel as we now have it, and it is this author that I will refer to as "John."

By the last decade of the first century, the period in which most scholars believe John's Gospel was written, the Gospels of Mark, Matthew and Luke were already in circulation in the known world. The evangelist may have used the Gospel of Mark as a source, but if so, he most certainly used it to a much lesser degree than did Matthew and Luke. It is more likely that John had access to another tradition similar to that of the Synoptic Gospels but different, a tradition that was independent of the other three Gospels.

Although there are similarities between the Synoptic Gospels and the Gospel of John, the differences between them are significant. For example, in the Synoptic Gospels, the greater part of Jesus' public ministry takes place in Galilee over what appears to be a one-year peri-od, and Jesus goes down to Jerusalem only once for Passover, during which the Passion takes place. In John's Gospel, however, Jesus' ministry is carried out in both Judea and Galilee and spans a period of at least three years. There are many miracles in the Synoptic Gospels, but in John's Gospel, there are only seven miraculous deeds. In the Synoptic Gospels, people in the narratives do not know the identity of Jesus as God's Son until the end of the Gospel, while in John's Gospel, Jesus himself speaks repeatedly of his oneness with his Father and of his origins in heaven. The many exor-cisms recounted in the Synoptic Gospels are absent in the Gospel of John. In the Synoptic Gospels, the final meal is centered around the Eucharist; in John's Gospel, however, the Eucharist is absent from the final meal, while its meaning is elucidated in John 6.

The fourth evangelist has his own unique vocabulary. For example, he uses the phrase "the Jews" to refer to those persons, especially the religious authorities, who are in opposition to Jesus, a fact that may lead to misunderstanding if one does not remember that Jesus himself and his disciples were all Jews. Jesus frequently speaks of his "hour," meaning his sufferings, death and resurrection. Neither the Beloved Disciple (or "the disciple whom Jesus loved") nor the "mother of Jesus" is ever named in this Gospel.

Long discourses and dialogues that reflect the faith of the Johannine community replace the parables of the Synoptic Gospels. These discourses serve to interpret the meaning of Jesus' miraculous deeds and the significance of who Jesus is.

This Gospel inspires and fascinates anyone who studies it seriously. It is my prayer that as you delve into this great source of Christian tradition, you be filled with the Spirit so as to reap the rich fruits the Gospel of John has to offer.

Journey 1
The Revelation of God's Son

Words are powerful: they can comfort or hurt; they can call forth the best in a person or make a person shrink in despair. Words can be empty or filled with deep meaning. Words tell us something about the person who speaks them; in that sense they are a means of revelation about the person.

Discovering

Read John 5:19-24.[1]
What do Jesus' words reveal about him?

Discovering

Read the prologue, John 1:1-18.
Name five important things we know about Jesus Christ from these lines.

Trace the journey of the Word in the prologue.

Exploring

The early Christians reflected on the meaning of Jesus' life, death and resurrection in light of the Old Testament. They did not view Jesus as one who started a new religion or brought about a break with Judaism and its religious traditions. Rather, they understood the Christ event as the great climax of God's plan to save us. Jesus was the fulfillment of God's promises to humanity throughout the Old Testament. Such reasoning is reflected in the introduction to the Gospel of John, the section known as the prologue (John 1:1-18).

In Genesis 1, God's word calls forth creation. God's goodness and love for us was first revealed through creative activity brought about by God's word. In the prophetical writings, God's will for the people and God's longing for loving response from the people is revealed through the prophets. Yet all these words were not enough to communicate fully God's great love for us and how God wished to be known and loved by us. Only in Jesus, God's "Word," was this revelation of God and God's great love for us finally made complete.

At the beginning of John's Gospel, the author speaks of this final revelation of God in Jesus as the "Word," which is personified in a similar way in the Old Testament Book of Wisdom. In John 1:17, the Word is identified as Jesus Christ.

The journey you have discovered is that of Jesus Christ as John expresses it throughout the Gospel.

Exploring

The Gospel of John has no infancy narrative as do the Gospels of Matthew and Luke. The incarnation, that is, God becoming human and living in our midst, is presented differently in the Johannine prologue than in those two Gospels: "And the Word became flesh and lived among us" (1:14). The phrase "lived among us" reminds one of the Old Testament *sheken* (the dwelling place of God's presence among the people).

The author of the Fourth Gospel, then, wishes the reader to understand that Jesus is the *sheken*, the dwelling place of God. God became present in this world

---

[1] In Scripture citations the first number refers to the chapter; this number is followed by a colon and the next number(s) indicate the verse(s). For example, John 5:19-24 refers to the fifth chapter, verses 19-24, of the Gospel of John. A long dash separating two numbers indicates that the passage covers more than one chapter, for example Genesis 1:1—2:4 refers to chapter 1, verse 1, through chapter 2, verse 4, of the Book of Genesis.

in the person of Jesus who is now our link with the Father. For the Jewish Christians, it was clear that the Holy of Holies (that is, the Tabernacle in the Temple) was no longer the place of God's presence to them. Jesus had replaced that Jewish institution in being God's personal presence to us. The emphasis of this Gospel, then, is on the divinity of Jesus, though John does not fail to show that he is human as well.

Discovering

Take a few minutes to contemplate this great mystery of God's love for us made evident in Jesus' coming. Where is God most intimately present to us in the risen Christ today?

Read the prologue again and notice the rhythm it has even in English.

Exploring

The words of this prologue, minus the verses about the testimony of John the Baptist, are thought to be an early Christian hymn. The fourth evangelist probably saw in this hymn a summary of the way he wished to present Jesus. Therefore, it serves as an introduction to the Gospel. On reading this prologue, one can easily foresee that John will stress the divinity of Jesus while not neglecting his humanity.

Discovering

Reread the prologue leaving out verses 6-8 and 15 in order to perceive the poetic beauty of this early Christian hymn. By so doing, one can almost recapture the joy of the early Church at worship after the resurrection and ascension of Jesus.

Exploring

In John's prologue (John 1:1-18), notice that Jesus is referred to as the "light" that shines in the "darkness." This dualistic language (referring to symbols that express negative and positive realitites), which is so typi-

cal of John's writing, distinguishes those in the Gospel who accept Jesus from those who are his opponents. The reader is challenged to be of the "light" and not of "darkness"; to live as one "from above" and not "from below"; to be of the "spirit" and not of the "flesh"; to live as people of the "truth" as Jesus enabled us to be rather than to be people of "falsehood."

Discovering

Note the positive and negative poles (dualistic vocabulary) and the meaning of the following verses:

John 1:5

negative:

positive:

meaning:

John 3:6

negative:

positive:

meaning:

John 3:31

negative:

positive:

meaning:

John 8:23

negative:

positive:

meaning:

John 3:36

negative:

positive:

meaning:

John 8:44-47
(keep in mind the person(s) to whom Jesus is speaking):

negative:

positive:

meaning:

Exploring

In the Synoptic Gospels, Jesus praises John the Baptist and identifies his role with that of Elijah. Elijah, according to Malachi 4:5-6, was to precede the "day of the Lord," the event of God's dramatic intervention in history in order to establish the reign of God on earth. But in the Fourth Gospel, John the Baptist makes no claims for himself other than that of preparing the way for the Lord. John 1:6-8 of the prologue states that John's role was to testify to the identity of Jesus. John gives testimony to Jesus' role as "Lamb of God." To understand the meaning of this title, we must look to the Old Testament. The blood of the Passover lamb saved the Israelites from the angel of death preceding their exodus from Egypt (Exodus 12:21-23). The early Christians understood Jesus in light of that event as the replacement of the Passover sacrifice. No longer was the blood of the Passover lamb their salvation; Jesus' own blood was the saving sacrifice for the sins of the world.

Perhaps as the early Church pondered the Old Testament prophecies, they also understood Jesus to be the faithful servant of God who, according to Isaiah, was led like an innocent lamb to the slaughter:

He was oppressed, and he was afflicted,
yet he did not open his mouth;
like a lamb that is led to the slaughter,
and like a sheep that is silent before its shearers is
    silent,...
yet he bore the sins of many,
and made intercession for the transgressors
    (Isaiah 53:7, 12).

In the passion narrative of this Gospel, the author mentions that Jesus' judgment under Pilate took place at noon (John 19:13-16). Anyone familiar with Jewish ritual would know that was the hour when the priests in the Temple began the slaughter of the Passover lambs. The Lamb of God was sentenced to death. Once again, Jesus is connected with the lamb of sacrifice for our sins.

The testimony that John the Baptist gave was revolutionary and dangerous. Basically, he was saying that the Jewish ritual was no longer necessary, that Jesus, not the paschal lamb, was to take away the sins of humanity. Moreover, in the latter part of his testimony, he testifies that Jesus is the Son of God. Yet when the religious leaders asked for credentials, John the Baptist made no claims for himself; he was not Elijah nor was he a prophet sent by God. His role was to draw attention not to himself but to Jesus and to bring people to the realization of who Jesus was.

Discovering

Read John 1:19-34. Read John 3:22-30.

What testimony does John the Baptist give concerning Jesus?

In the space below, write three ways you may be challenged to give testimony to your belief in Jesus and his teachings today. Then write a brief prayer for honesty and courage to testify to your identity as a Christian—that is, a follower of Christ—by the way you live and speak.

1.

2.

3.

Prayer:

Discovering

Even though parts of the Gospel of John may be difficult to understand, it is important that you read the whole Gospel in order to get a sense of the way John presents the life, death and resurrection of Jesus. One or more of the following techniques may assist you in reading the Gospel:

- The Gospel is long, and it may be necessary to read it in two sittings—chapters 1—12 and chapters 13—21. If you are doing this study with a group, you may want to read the Gospel aloud, with individuals taking the following parts: narrator, the Jews, other characters.
- Take note of words, phrases and ideas that occur repeatedly throughout the Gospel. This will take a lot of time, but it is necessary to get a sense of the story and how it differs from the other Gospels.
- Keep this question in mind as you read the Gospel: Who is Jesus as presented by John?

Looking Back

On Journey 1 you made the following discoveries:

- The early Church used the Old Testament Scriptures to reflect on the meaning of Jesus' life, death and resurrection.
- The prologue to John's Gospel introduces the story of Jesus as presented by the fourth evangelist: Jesus came down from the Father and dwelt among us, was rejected and killed and returned in glory to the Father.
- Jesus is called the "Word" by John because he communicates who God is to us.
- The prologue was probably an early Christian hymn, which John used to introduce his Gospel.
- John used dualistic vocabulary to emphasize the clarity with which the reader must make his or her choice for Jesus and his teaching.
- John's role was to give testimony about Jesus.

Exploring Further

Brown, Raymond E. *The Gospel and Epistles of John: A Concise Commentary.* Collegeville, Minn.: The Liturgical Press, 1988.

Kysar, Robert. *John: the Maverick Gospel.* Atlanta: John Knox Press, 1976.

Journey 2
Two Signs at Cana

In the last journey, you studied the prologue to John's Gospel. You were informed that the Word of God is said to be God, that he became human and that he was rejected by his people. You also learned that this hymn probably emerged from the Christian community that perceived the glory of God manifested in Jesus. We were prepared by the prologue for the rest of the Gospel, that is, to see Jesus as both divine and human. In this journey, we will see how the glory of God, present in Jesus, was first shown in his miraculous deed at Cana.

Discovering

Read Psalm 66:5; Psalm 77:12; Deuteronomy 3:24.

In these passages, what are the wondrous works of God? Indicate some ways in which God continues to work in your life. Spend some time giving thanks to God in your heart.

Read John 5:16-1, 36; 14:10.

What do these passages tell us about Jesus and his miraculous deeds?

Exploring

In the Gospel of John, Jesus most often refers to his wondrous deeds as "works," whereas other people within the Gospel allude to his miracles as "signs." The author seems to have borrowed this terminology from the Old Testament. Both "signs" and "works" are found in the Old Testament in relation to the exodus.

First, we will explore the meaning of "works" as Jesus uses it in John's Gospel. In the Book of Exodus, God uses "works" to refer to his saving deeds in delivering the Hebrews from slavery under the Egyptian Pharaoh: "Before all your people I will perform marvels [works], such as have not been performed in all the earth or in any nation; and all the people among whom you live may see the work of the LORD: for it is an awesome thing that I will do to you" (Exodus 34:10). Therefore, by the use of the word *works* for his marvelous deeds, Jesus identifies himself with the God of the Old Testament who continues to do great "works" in Jesus for God's people. The word *works* emphasizes Jesus' miraculous deeds from God's perspective. It is fitting therefore that Jesus, who is one with the Father, calls them "works."

But "works" also has a broader sense; Jesus speaks of his whole ministry, both his words and deeds, as "works": "I glorified you on earth by finishing the work that you gave me to do" (John 17:4). In other words, in everything Jesus says and does, God is at work in him bringing about the divine will for human beings.

Discovering

How do each of the following passages express the power of God? In each case, who are the people who respond in faith?

Read John 2:1-11.

Read John 4:46-54.

Read John 5:1-47.

Exploring

That which Jesus alludes to as "works" in the Gospel, other people refer to as "signs." The word *sign* shares with the word *work* the same Old Testament background. For example, God acts on behalf of the people in the exodus event to save them from destruction. In speaking of the miraculous deeds on their behalf as signs, God tells Moses that the purpose of the signs is "that they may know that I am the Lord" (Exodus 10:1-2). The signs were to direct the people's attention to God's power acting on their account.

The signs in this Gospel, then, are to direct the reader's attention to the glory of God, spoken of in the prologue (John 1:14) and made manifest in Jesus' miraculous deeds. Jesus is more than just a man, the signs tell us; in him we encounter the eternal "I AM."

We can see that the word *work* emphasizes that God is at work in Jesus, whereas *sign* stresses the human view of Jesus' miraculous deeds. Signs in John's Gospel are in fact miraculous deeds, as are "works," but the expression "sign" also brings into focus a symbolic meaning. A sign points beyond the deed to something significant about Jesus' identity so as to evoke a response of faith in the witnesses. In fact, John states near the end of the Gospel: "Now Jesus did many other signs in the presence of his disciples, which are not written in this book. But these are written so that you may come to believe that Jesus is the Messiah, the Son of God, and that through believing you may have life in his name" (John 20:30-31). Most often the symbolism becomes more obvious in the dialogue or monologue that follows the miraculous deed.

Discovering

Read Exodus 3:1-15; 10:1-2.

How is John 2:1-11 related to these passages from Exodus?

what way will Jesus' hour affect those who believe in him?

Read John 4:21.

Read John 5:28-29.

Read John 16:2.

Read John 16:25.

Read John 2:12-25. Spend some time praying with this text in the silence of your heart. What are the requirements for eternal life?

Discovering

The following passages speak of "an hour." They seem to indicate that the results of Jesus' hour will affect those who believe in him. In the following passages, in

Exploring

According to John, Jesus worked two miracles at Cana. This first miraculous deed occurred at a wedding feast; Jesus changed the water in six stone water jars into wine when the wine ran out. His mother, never named in this Gospel, is mentioned only one other time—at the foot of the cross (John 19:25-27). Thus John ties the wedding feast at Cana to the crucifixion.

John's intention is that his readers see more than just the miraculous deed; he wants them to look beyond the sign to see who Jesus is and what the sign says about him. In order to do that, we must look at the symbols and what they signify in relation to Jesus. In the late first century B.C., wine had become for the Jews a symbol associated with the coming of the Messiah. Isaiah and other prophets had expressed the appearance of a messiah, a descendant of David, in terms of abundant wine (Isaiah 25:26; Amos 9:11; Joel 3:18). This sign worked at Cana, then, confirmed that Jesus was indeed the Messiah.

By connecting the abundance of wine with the presence of his mother, who will appear only once more in this Gospel at the foot of the cross, John directs his readers to understand that Jesus' messiahship or kingship is not political. Rather, Jesus' glory is not to be thought of in terms of earthly trappings of a king.

Instead, he will manifest his glory on the cross, where the "King of the Jews" gives his life for all. Jesus indicates to his mother that his "hour has not yet come." The "hour" in John's Gospel most frequently refers to Jesus' sufferings and death. Later in the Gospel, Jesus tells the Greeks who come to see him: "The hour has come for the Son of Man to be glorified" (John 12:20-23).

The stone jars are a reminder of the Jewish purification rites. By Jesus' transformation of the water into wine, we learn that Jesus replaced the purification rites with his own death on the cross, which would transform our sinfulness into faith.

The scene that follows, usually called the "Cleansing of the Temple" (2:12-25), takes Jesus to Jerusalem, where he carries through with the theme that he himself becomes the focus of God's presence, rather than the Temple and its rituals. He drives out the animals that were used for sacrifice. Then, in his conversation with the woman of Samaria whom he encountered at Jacob's well (4:4-42), Jesus tells her that he has replaced both worship in Jerusalem and worship on Mount Gerizim.

Discovering

Read John 4:46-54.

The reader is challenged to an outstanding faith such as that of the royal official. On what basis does the man believe? Can you relate a time when you faced a great challenge to your faith in Jesus' power?

Write a brief prayer for the kind of faith Jesus asks of us.

Exploring

Back in Galilee, Jesus works his second miracle (John 4:46-54) in the same town of Cana where he worked his first one. A royal official asks Jesus to heal his son. Without seeing the boy, Jesus heals him at a distance and tells the father to return home, that his son lives. This miracle stresses both faith and Jesus' power to give life. Faith, as a positive reaction to Jesus, was emphasized in the previous chapters. Now the royal official is set forth as a model for faith; he does not require the sign before he believes in Jesus.

The second theme, also accentuated in chapters 2 through 4, is that Jesus has power to give life. He spoke of eternal life to Nicodemus and connected it with faith (3:14-15). To the Samaritan woman, Jesus spoke of living water "welling up to eternal life" (5:13-16, 36). Now he assures the boy's father that his sick child will live. Thus we are introduced to the theme of life that will follow in the rest of the Gospel (i.e., "the bread of life" in 6:1-71, "the living water" in 7:37-39 and "the light of life" in 8:12). The theme of life will climax with Jesus' resurrection.

Looking Back

On Journey 2 you made the following discoveries:

- The word *works* designates Jesus' miraculous deeds and focuses on God at work in Jesus. *Signs* focuses our attention on who this person is who works such wondrous deeds.
- The sign at the wedding feast in Cana reminds us that Jesus is the Messiah who sacrifices his life for our sins.
- The royal official's faith, based solely on Jesus' word that he had healed his son, challenges the reader to believe without seeing.

Exploring Further

Collins, Raymond F. *John and His Witness.* Zacchaeus Studies: New Testament. Collegeville, Minn.: Michael Glazier/The Liturgical Press, 1991.

Journey 3
Darkness and Light, Midnight and Noon

Most of us have seen the leaves of a green plant turn yellow for lack of sunlight and then begin to fall. The majority of plants require light to live and grow. Human beings, too, need light for healthy living. In the Gospel of John, light and life are associated with Jesus, while darkness and death are associated with evil or Satan. In this journey, we will see that on encountering Jesus, one must accept Jesus as the light of life if one wishes to live.

Discovering

Read John 3:1-21.
   What seems to be the evangelist's intention for telling us that Nicodemus went to Jesus "in the night"?

To what do the symbols "night" (3:2) and "darkness" (3:19-21) refer?

What do verses 19-21 tell us about Nicodemus?

How does a Christian experience being "born from above"?

Exploring

Nicodemus, a leader among the Jews and a Pharisee, probably a member of the Sanhedrin, goes in the night (that is, the darkness) to see Jesus (John 3:1-21). In contrast to the royal official's faith, Nicodemus' faith is inadequate in that his belief in Jesus is not based on Jesus' word about who he is and where he comes from but rather on the signs Jesus worked. Nicodemus sees Jesus merely as another rabbi of Israel who can work miracles. He fails to understand that Jesus came to earth from God in order that we might be born into eternal life. Jesus tells Nicodemus that "no one can see the kingdom of God without being born from above" (John 3:3). Since Jesus came from above and is one with the Father, he has the power to give life from above. The Greek word for "above" also means "again"; Nicodemus understands the latter meaning and hence focuses on the impossibility of entering the womb again. Even though he is a teacher, Nicodemus remains in the darkness and depicts the darkness referred to in the prologue, which did not comprehend the light (John 1:5).
   If you were unable to answer any of the questions in the previous "Discovering" section, go back and answer them.

Discovering

Read John 4:1-42.
   Then reread verses 5 through 15. Compare the woman's reaction to Jesus with that of Nicodemus.

What do you understand by the "living water"?

Exploring

The woman whom Jesus encounters at the well in Samaria has a very different background from that of Nicodemus. This unnamed woman was a Samaritan, whereas Nicodemus was a Jew. As a woman married so many times and a Samaritan (a person of mixed blood—Jewish and Gentile), she would be considered a marginal person.

In contrast, Nicodemus was a well-respected member of Jewish society. The time of the meeting with Jesus in each case was different also—the woman encounters Jesus at noon, whereas Nicodemus goes to Jesus at night.

The well may be a reminder that before meeting Rebekah at a well, Jacob had a dream of a ladder that reached from earth to heaven; angels climbed up and down the ladder (Genesis 28). The angels, a symbol of communication between God and earth, are now replaced by Jesus, who is God's communication with us.

When Jesus asks the woman for a drink, she questions why Jesus, a Jew, would humble himself to ask a Samaritan for a drink. Jesus responds that if she had known who he was, she would have asked him for a drink of living water, a water far surpassing that which she drew from the well. Just as Nicodemus misunderstood Jesus' statements about birth from above, the woman likewise misunderstands Jesus' references to spiritual needs as referring to physical needs. But she continues to engage Jesus in conversation. She appears willing to listen to him, and she even asks for that of which she has no understanding—the living water of which Jesus speaks.

Discovering

Read John 4:16-26.
What effect does this woman's witness have?

What other witnesses to Jesus have we encountered thus far in the Gospel of John?

Exploring

When the woman continues to misunderstand, Jesus tells her about her past life; he is indeed someone greater than she has suspected. But the woman cleverly changes the subject when Jesus challenges her about the six men she has had. She tests Jesus' tolerance by bringing up an age-old issue of theological and national importance—should people worship in the Samaritan holy place on Mount Gerizim or in the Temple at Jerusalem? Worship had long been controversial for the Samaritans. They were of mixed blood, the Jews of Samaria having intermarried with pagan people. In 721 B.C., the Assyrians conquered other nations with whom the Samaritans intermarried.

Jesus does not choose between the two alternatives the woman gives him; rather, he responds that the day is coming when true worship will replace both the holy place on Mount Gerizim and the Jerusalem Temple. Not only will Jesus replace the ritual cleansing waters as symbolized in the wedding feast at Cana, but he will also replace the Temple. Henceforth, the focus of worship will be in Jesus; the Spirit will give life that will empower people to worship God properly in Jesus.

The woman then makes an observation about a Messiah who would come and show them all things (John 4:25). Jesus in turn reveals his identity to her; he is that Messiah. She immediately goes back to her village and gives witness to Jesus. Because of the testimony of this woman, many of the Samaritans came to believe in Jesus. Belief for John is much more than an intellectual acceptance; "belief" in this Gospel implies a total commitment of oneself to Jesus and all that he does and teaches. This woman brought the Samaritan people to this kind of faith.

Looking Back

On Journey 3 you made the following discoveries:

- "Night" in this Gospel is symbolic of incomprehension and, in some cases, rejection.
- Nicodemus represents those people who do not believe Jesus' word concerning his identity, as well as people who hear Jesus' word but do not comprehend it.
- The symbol of living water of which Jesus speaks represents God's gifts in and through Jesus.
- John stresses the theme of faith in Jesus as the source of life. "Faith" in the Gospel of John implies a total commitment to Jesus and all that he teaches.

Exploring Further

Brown, Raymond E. *The Gospel According to John (I-XII)*, Anchor Bible Series. Garden City, N.Y.: Doubleday & Company, 1966.

Journey 4

Healing for the Lame, Food for the Hungry

When I was a child, I waited for two events each year—Christmas and my birthday. I would think about them months in advance and ask my mother time and time again, "How long is it now till Christmas?" and "When is my birthday coming?" People wait for many things—some wait in prisons for years to pass so that they may be released; others wait for their economic situation to take a turn for the better; some wait eagerly for the conception of a child. Sometimes when the waiting goes on too long, we grow tired of waiting and begin to accept that things will stay as they are.

Discovering

Read John 5:1-9.

Is there anything surprising to you in this story? Why?

Have you ever waited for something for such a long time that you became weary? Recall that event. If you prayed for it, did you give up praying, or did you continue to pray?

God alone can fill our ultimate desires.

Exploring

The man whom Jesus cured at the Pool of Bethesda waited thirty-eight years for healing. His ancestors had also waited thirty-eight years in the desert for God to fulfill his promises of a land for them (Deuteronomy 2:14). Strangely, after the man at Bethesda waited all those years, it is Jesus who asks the crippled man if he wants to be healed, not the reverse. The man simply waited at the pool for a mysterious bubbling to occur. According to his belief, the healing powers were effective only if one were the first to be immersed in the pool when the water bubbled.

When Jesus, without making any demands, asks if he wishes to be healed, the man simply responds with his belief in the magical moment of immersion. He asks nothing of Jesus; he has lost all hope. This man does not have the faith of the royal official who asked for his son's cure (John 4:46-54). Yet, Jesus tells the man to rise and take up his mat and walk. Jesus heals the man, and he does it on the Sabbath, thereby breaking the Jewish law. The man picked up his mat and walked as Jesus commanded him, but there was no sign of faith which, in this Gospel, demands a total commitment of one's life to Jesus and his words. Jesus was willing to take the risk of helping another no matter what it might cost him with the religious leaders.

Discovering

Read John 5:10-18.

Contrast the actions of Jesus with those of the man who was healed.

Contrast Jesus' act with the desire of Jesus' enemies.

What are some ways in which we sometimes act in the manner of the healed man and the enemies of Jesus?

Exploring

Later when Jesus found the man in the Temple area, he told him to sin no more, for it was also important that the man be healed spiritually. However, the sign Jesus worked did not evoke faith in the healed man. His lack of faith is obvious when he goes out and "rats" on Jesus. "The Jews" (those in opposition to Jesus who was himself a Jew) challenge him concerning his breaking the Sabbath by carrying his mat. The man responds, "The man who healed me said, 'Take up your mat and walk'" (John 5:11). Jesus was no more than a mere man to this person who had just been restored to full health after thirty-eight years. The healing had not brought him to commit himself to Jesus.

How strange that "the Jews" would not rejoice that the man had been healed after waiting so many years! But John tells us that they began to persecute Jesus because he had performed this act on the Sabbath. Thus the man wittingly or unwittingly draws Jesus into a debate with his enemies over observance of the Sabbath. Jesus defends himself on the grounds that both his Father and he are at work. "The Jews" presumed that God works on the Sabbath since people are born and people die. The implication was clear—Jesus was equating himself with God who alone has the right to work on the Sabbath. "For this reason the Jews were seeking all the more to kill him" (John 5:18). They wanted to take away life from the one who had given full life to a crippled person.

Discovering

Following the cure of the lame man, John gives us his account of the multiplication of the loaves and fishes.

Read John 6:1-15.

What did the feast of Passover commemorate?

Where was Jesus when he worked the miracle?

Compare John's account of the multiplication of the loaves with Mark 6:32-44 in respect to the following:

Who has the five loaves?

John

Mark

Compare the details in John 6:11 with Mark 5:41, paying close attention to the subject and the verbs.

John

Mark

Read 2 Kings 4:42.

Read Isaiah 49:8-10 and Exodus 16.

Exploring

Opposition from Jesus' enemies begins to ferment even more with the multiplication of the loaves in Galilee near the feast of Passover. Jesus has already made himself equal to God by healing the crippled man on the Sabbath; now he will feed five thousand people with five loaves and two fish and claim to be the bread of life that has the power to give eternal life.

John's account of the multiplication of the loaves replaces the Synoptic account of the institution of the Eucharist during the Last Supper. Several details, especially the verbs used in John's account, are reminiscent of the eucharistic meal: "Then Jesus took the loaves, and when he had given thanks [*eucharistesas* in Greek, which is similar to our English word *eucharist*], he [not the disciples as in the Synoptic Gospels] distributed them to those who were seated" (John 6:11).

There are obvious motifs from the exodus event (Exodus 16): the mention that the miraculous feeding takes place on a mountain (reminiscent of Sinai), the gathering of the fragments (reminiscent of gathering the manna in the desert), the murmurings of the crowds in the discourse that follows in John 6:41, 60 (the people murmur or complain about the manna in the desert). By casting the early Church tradition of the Eucharist within the tradition of Jesus' feeding of the five thousand, John was able to make an important theological implication—God gave his people manna to rescue them from death by hunger in the desert; now God, present in Jesus, has come to earth to give his people the bread of eternal life.

Discovering

Read John 1:16-24.
    Read Psalm 107:23-32. What likeness do you find in these two readings?

Exploring

In relating the story of Jesus walking on the water between the account of the feeding (John 6:1-15) and the discourse on the bread of life (John 6:25-61), John wants to affirm for his readers the identity of this Jesus who came from the Father to live among us. He is Lord over all nature just as Yahweh showed himself to be in the crossing of the Red Sea after the Israelites were led out of Egypt. The literal translation of the Greek is: "Do not be afraid. I AM" (John 6:20). Most translations give us "I am he," but a literal translation of the Greek is "I AM," the divine name of Yahweh that was revealed to Moses in the Exodus event.

Discovering

Read John 6:25-71.
    What are the motives of the crowd that seeks Jesus?

Exploring

The crowd had gotten a free meal, and they come back for more. They have not understood who Jesus is, and they focus on the natural instead of the supernatural, that which is not of this world. Jesus makes three claims; the responses he receives show the crowd's lack of faith: "I am the bread of life" (6:35). The Jews murmur because he made this claim (6:41). "Whoever eats of this bread will live forever; and the bread that I will give for the life of the world is my flesh" (6:51). The Jews quarrel among themselves because Jesus offered them his flesh to eat, which appears absurd to them (6:52). "Those who eat my flesh and drink my blood have eternal life (6:54);...this is the bread that came down from heaven" (6:58). His disciples murmur (6:61), and many "turned back and no longer went about with him" (6:66).

When Jesus asks the Twelve if they, too, wished to leave him, Peter shows himself as the spokesperson for the rest who have faith: He understands that Jesus alone can give life: "Lord, to whom can we go? You have the words of eternal life" (6:68).

Jesus responds that one of them would betray him (6:70-71). This pattern follows the institution of the Eucharist in the Gospel of Luke—the institution of the Eucharist followed by Jesus' prediction of Judas's betrayal (Luke 22:21-23).

Discovering

How important is the Eucharist to you? How do you show your love for Christ in the Eucharist?

Belief in the Eucharist as the risen Christ's body and blood (Jesus' expression for giving himself to us in intimate communion) demands faith. Take a few minutes to sit quietly in deep gratitude for the gift of faith that you have.

Looking Back

On Journey 4 you made the following discoveries:

- The miraculous deeds Jesus worked in this Gospel were meant to evoke faith.
- Faith in Jesus as presented in the Gospel of John means a total commitment to Jesus and all that he says.
- John shows us that Jesus is the presence of Yahweh among us and that presence remains among us in the Eucharist in which Jesus gives us himself in intimate union.
- Betrayal by one who follows Jesus is always possible if one does not cling to him in faith.

Exploring Further

Karris, Robert J. *Jesus and the Marginalized in John's Gospel.* Zacchaeus Studies: New Testament. Collegeville, Minn.: Michael Glazier/The Liturgical Press, 1990.

Yee, Gale A. *Jewish Feasts and the Gospel of John.* Wilmington, Del.: Michael Glazier, 1989.

Journey 5

Who Really Is Blind?

When I was teaching in college, Susan, a person blind from birth, used to come to class with her seeing-eye dog, Bumps. Just as I would utter a most profound statement that I was sure would "wow" the class, Bumps would come forth with a human-like groan of boredom. Susan told me that he would do that frequently right at the punch line when she was watching TV. "If you don't mind my asking," I said, "how do you watch TV?" "I sit in front of it and look at the screen in my mind." She proceeded to tell me about a program we had both watched the night before. I was astounded at the details she had picked up that I had missed. It made me wonder which of us was really blind.

Discovering

Read John 9:1-41.
  How does the story begin?

How does it end?

This story of the man born blind is an example of Johannine drama at its best. There are seven "scenes" in the story. Who are the characters in each scene? Write the characters and what happens in each scene in the spaces provided.

1.

2.

3.

4.

5.

6.

7.

Read John 1:19-34; 3:22-36.
Summarize in your own words John the Baptist's witness to Jesus.

Exploring

A prevalent idea in the first century was that the fortunate people in this world were good and, because of their goodness, God had blessed them. The unfortunate ones, it was thought, were being punished because of sin. Even today, many people reflect that mistaken notion when they have to deal with some difficulty or tragedy. Jesus, however, dispels their assumption that it was either the blind man or else his parents who had sinned. Rather, Jesus explained, God's glory would be manifested through the misfortune of this man.

Jesus' declaration, "I am the light of the world" (John 8:12), alerts us to the theme of light that is developed in 9:1-41. The story begins with the blind man who comes to see as a result of Jesus' healing. It ends with the Pharisees who think they see, but who in reality have plunged themselves deeper into darkness.

Discovering

Many Old Testament prophecies dealt with the coming of the messiah and his accomplishments. Read Isaiah 29:18; 35:5; 42:6-7. What light do these passages cast on the story of the man born blind?

Read John 1:35-51.
In what way do Andrew and Philip witness to Jesus?

Take some time to reflect on the faith of this man who was born blind. In this Gospel, faith means a personal and active commitment to Jesus. How does the man demonstrate an active commitment in the story?

Ponder your own commitment to Jesus. In what ways could you show more commitment to him?

Write a prayer of resolve to be more actively committed to Jesus in your everyday life.

Exploring

The story focuses on several themes. One of the themes is the triumph of light over darkness, that is, Jesus' triumph over evil or sin. In the Old Testament, the prophets frequently used prophetic actions to demonstrate their message. Jesus does the same in the account of this healing; the healing of physical blindness illustrates the reality that Jesus is indeed the light of the world who came to heal its spiritual blindness.

Another theme is the Sabbath question. Instead of rejoicing with the man who now sees, the Pharisees become indignant because Jesus healed the man on the Sabbath. The problem lies in the fact that Jesus spat on the ground, made mud with the spittle and rubbed it on the man's eyes. Kneading was not allowed on the Sabbath, and mixing a paste would fall into that category. Mixing mud with anything may have been a reminder of mixing clay with straw while they were enslaved in Egypt.

Witnessing to Jesus is another theme that stands out in this story. Various people, beginning with John the Baptist, Andrew and Philip, witness to Jesus in this Gospel. Like them, every Christian is called to evangelize (that is, to make Jesus known to others through the way we live our lives and what we say). The man who now sees makes a series of witnesses. In the first witness, he tells the neighbors in simple terms Jesus' name and what he did for him (John 9:8-12). Then he witnesses to the Pharisees; he repeats what Jesus did and, in answering their accusations that Jesus couldn't be from God because he broke the Sabbath, the man questions their own wisdom and states that Jesus is a prophet (John 9:13-17). His parents are afraid to witness because of threat of expulsion from the synagogue. This was probably a challenge to timid Christians in the 80's. Again he witnesses to belief in Jesus in 9:24-34 and states his belief in Jesus as a man from God. In a brief dialogue with Jesus later on, the man makes his confession: "'Lord, I believe.' And he worshiped him" (John 9:38).

Therefore, we see in this simple man one who could not see the light of day, but opens himself to see the light of the world. The Pharisees, on the other hand, see the light of day, but close themselves to Jesus, the light of the world. In their stubbornness of heart, they prefer the darkness and refuse to enter the light.

Looking Back

On Journey 5 you made the following discoveries:

- The story of the man born blind is presented in a form somewhat like a minidrama in seven scenes.
- When Jesus opened the eyes of the man born blind, he proved himself to be the Messiah, who, according to Isaiah's prophecy, would open the eyes of the blind.
- The choice of light or darkness is offered to those called to be followers of Christ.
- Fear of expulsion from the synagogue was still an issue for some people in the Johannine community, a fear reflected in this story.
- Witness to Christ is important in this Gospel as a challenge to all who would follow him.

Exploring Further

Thompson, Marianne Meye. *The Incarnate Word: Perspectives on Jesus in the Fourth Gospel.* Peabody, Mass.: Hendrickson, 1988.

Journey 6

The Good Shepherd, the Giver of Life

"I am the good shepherd" (John 10:14). "A shepherd, huh? And a good one at that! Where do you find one of that caliber? Maybe a good priest, or a good rabbi, but a shepherd?" I can imagine the reaction of the crowds when Jesus compared himself to a shepherd. Shepherds were not well thought of in first-century society: They grazed their flocks on other people's land, and since they were in the fields day and night, they were probably dirty, and they couldn't observe the Jewish rituals. Jesus could raise eyebrows with one short statement. But he seemed to thrive on associations that shocked others, such as fellowship with people whom his Father alone seemed to care about.

Discovering

Read John 10:1-21.

Metaphors help us to understand a reality. Pick out the metaphors or images Jesus uses to describe himself. What does each one mean to you?

Who are some false shepherds today?

Exploring

In the last journey, we examined John's account of the man blind from birth. That event is related to Jesus' designation of himself as "the good shepherd." It is the good shepherd's compassion that led Jesus to heal the man. Now Jesus wants to make it clear to his listeners that he longs to extend that compassion and care to all people.

A sheepfold was an area in the field where the sheep grazed; it was encompassed by a wall of stones and protected the sheep from predators at night.

In this simple allegory, Jesus is the good shepherd; those who believe in him and love him are the sheep of his flock; the false shepherds are the enemies of Jesus who try to steal his kingdom. The sheep know the voice of the good shepherd because they have established an intimate relationship with him. In contrast, they will run from a false shepherd, that is, anyone who would try to take the place of Jesus in leading them.

Discovering

In what concrete way might you follow the good shepherd in today's society?

Read Ezekiel 34.

Notice the image of sheep used for the people of God in the Old Testament. How did Jesus fulfill that prophecy?

Take time to sit alone in the presence of the good shepherd. Hear him call you by name. Thank him for choosing you to be of his fold and for loving you so much as to lay down his life for you. Think of some time in your life when you may have chosen to belong to someone else's flock. Then hear Jesus call your name; imagine him taking you from a false shepherd, holding you in his arms and loving you into wholeness again.

Exploring

It seems important to Jesus that his listeners comprehend how much he wants to care for them, that they know he longs to be with them just as a shepherd remains with the flock day and night. Jesus' love for his sheep is so great that he lays down his life for them. When the people do not understand Jesus, he uses another allegory to explain the first. In John 10:7-10 and 11-16, Jesus identifies himself as the door of the sheepfold.

The sheepfold had only one opening or door through which the sheep could enter and leave. Jesus identifies himself as that door or opening. The flock must come and go through him, and only by so doing will the sheep know the Father and find nourishment. He is the only way to the Father; there is no other—not by sacrifices in the Temple, nor by ritual cleansings, nor by keeping the law does one enter God's flock, but only through Jesus.

Jesus also invites and challenges those who oppose him to enter the sheepfold through him. As their behavior has already demonstrated in the previous chapters of John's Gospel, they have been acting as false shepherds and thieves. They represent the darkness; they come to steal and slaughter and take away the life that only Jesus, who is light and life, can give.

There is but one shepherd, Jesus maintains, who is one with the Father. The oneness of Jesus with the Father must be reflected in the unity among the sheep under the leadership of the good shepherd.

Discovering

Why do the religious authorities want to kill Jesus? What are their main accusations?

Read John 17:1-26, Jesus' prayer for his disciples. Keep in mind that Jesus' "hour" is his death and resurrection. How is this passage similar to the allegory of the good shepherd?

Read the story of the raising of Lazarus (John 11:1-44). How does Jesus demonstrate that he is the good shepherd in this seventh sign?

What are the striking aspects of this story to you? Why?

Rewrite in your own words Martha's confession in John 11:28.

Go back and read about the response from the man who had been blind when Jesus reveals his identity to him (John 9:35-38). How does his response to Jesus compare with Martha's and Mary's responses to Jesus in 11:2-27 and 11:32?

Discovering

The more Jesus showed himself to be the light, the more those who preferred the darkness sought to take away the light and life of the world. Reread John 11:4-57. John's skill in use of irony is at play in this passage. In irony, a statement is made but its full truth is unknown to the speaker. One example in this passage is: "...[I]t is better for you to have one man die for the people..." (11:50). Actually, Caiaphas meant "in place of the people," when in truth, Jesus does die so that we may live. Can you find any other statements of irony in this passage or in other parts of the Gospel?

Exploring

Martha asks nothing of Jesus when he arrives after her brother had already died and been in the tomb four days. She simply states that the tomb would not have claimed her brother had Jesus been there with his friend. Jesus promises her that Lazarus will rise, but Martha interprets that to mean that he will rise on "the last day." To a woman who was mourning the loss of her brother, "the last day" seemed like a long time to wait. But Jesus' reply is that the eschatological event (that is, the endtime event of the coming of God in glory when the dead would rise) was already present in himself. The loving, trusting relationship between God and human beings was even now at work in Jesus.

When Mary goes to meet Jesus, she reiterates her sister's belief that Jesus' presence would have prevented her brother's death. Her weeping accompanied by the weeping of the people who went with her was then joined by Jesus' own tears. In this account of the raising of Lazarus, we see in no uncertain terms the humanity of Jesus who is also God and has power over life and death.

Four days in the tomb—there was no doubt that the man was dead. But Jesus, who proclaimed that he was the resurrection and the life, now demonstrates that even death is subordinate to the power of God at work in Jesus. Several phrases remind us of the power of death and Jesus' victory over it: "four days in the tomb"; "Take away the stone"; "Lazarus, come forth"; "Unbind him" (John 11:39, 43, 44). Never again would death claim the final victory.

Exploring

Caiaphas' fear (John 11:50) was based on Roman violent suppression of prophetic movements in the past that had caused unrest among the Jews. John, writing in the latter part of the first century, knew of the military action against some insurrectionists in Palestine in his own lifetime that ended with the destruction of the Temple in A.D. 70.

Looking Back

On Journey 6 you made the following discoveries:

- In Jesus, God fulfilled the promise made through Ezekiel: "I myself shall be the shepherd of my sheep" (Ezekiel 34:15).
- In the raising of Lazarus from the dead, the good shepherd demonstrated his loving care for his friend, Lazarus, and thus prefigured his own resurrection from the dead.
- Both the allegory of the good shepherd and the raising of Lazarus demonstrated that Jesus initiated the eschatological event of God's intimate relationship with us.
- When Jesus revealed his identity to the man born blind and later to Martha, then to Mary, their responses demonstrated the belief and response of the ideal Christian.

Exploring Further

Comblin, Jose. *Sent From the Father. Meditations on the Fourth Gospel*. Maryknoll, N.Y.: Orbis Books, 1979.

Countryman, William. *The Mystical Way in the Fourth Gospel*. Revised edition. Valley Forge, Pa.: Trinity Press, 1994.

Journey 7
The King Is Anointed and Enters the Holy City

In Journey 6, you saw Lazarus' resurrection as a fore-shadowing of Jesus' own resurrection, as well as a motivation for Jesus' enemies to determine that he must die. Now we begin our study of the events directly associated with Jesus' hour of glory.

Discovering

Read John 12:1-6.

When does the anointing take place? How does this connect the story with Jesus' death?

How does Mary compare with Judas in this story of the anointing?

How does Judas compare with the enemies of the good shepherd in John 10:7-10?

Compare the anointing in the Gospel of John with Mark 14:1-9?

Holy persons through the ages have been extravagant in their demonstration of love for the Lord. Each of us is called in Baptism to be holy. How might you show your extravagant love for Jesus in today's world?

Exploring

In the raising of Lazarus, we saw that Jesus' enemies determined that death was the answer to their problem with Jesus. Once again our attention is drawn to his death in the anointing scene—the betrayer is mentioned and Jesus speaks of Mary's act of love as preparation for his burial. The Greek word used for "dinner" indicates a climate of joy and celebration with friends. The anointing of Jesus' feet might have added to that celebration had it not been a symbol of burial and had Judas been able to celebrate instead of focusing on his greed.

In the Greco-Roman world, hosts would generally provide water and sometimes oil for guests, because in a world where sandals were worn and the soil was dry and dusty, washing and anointing were soothing to the feet. But in general, one did one's own footwashing and anointing. Only a slave might be expected to wash and anoint another's feet. In Homer's *Odyssey*, upon Odysseus' return home, his nurse and slave since childhood recognized him, in spite of his disguise, when she washed his feet and saw an old scar on his leg.

The anointing of Jesus' feet, then, portrays Mary's great love and devotion to Jesus; she was implying that she would willingly be his slave.

When Mary poured the perfume upon the feet of Jesus, the house was filled with the fragrance of the pound of costly perfume, an extravagance of perfume, both in amount and quality, fit for a king. "Pure nard" (John 12:3), as the perfume was called, was an imported aromatic herb estimated by Judas to be valued at three hundred denarii, a sum equal to about ten months' wages for a common laborer.

In the ancient world a woman's hair was a symbol of the dignity she bore, so women in general were very careful of their hair and most always wore it long. Damaged hair was considered degrading. Mary, however, wipes the feet of Jesus with her hair. Hair was symbolic of the whole person (see 1 Samuel 14:45; Judges 13:5; 16:17, 19-22). Thus Mary, in wiping the feet of Jesus with her hair, gives her total self in love for her Lord—indeed, an ideal disciple. Her act of love for Jesus is paralleled and surpassed by Jesus' humble act of love at the Last Supper when he washes his disciples' feet and later gives his life out of love.

Discovering

Read John 12:9-11.
 What does it mean to believe or to have faith in Jesus? (If you do not remember the idea conveyed by the Greek word for "belief" or "faith" in this Gospel, turn back to Journey 3.)

In view of the meaning of "belief" in Greek, rephrase John 12:10-11.

Exploring

Darkness seems to be gaining momentum as hatred for Jesus and his signs increases. The Sanhedrin has already decided that the one who is the resurrection and the life must die (11:53). Now they decide that Lazarus, the one Jesus raised from the dead, must be put back into the tomb because many people were believing in Jesus. Indeed Jesus' testimony that the world's works were evil (John 3:20; 7:7) is obviously crystallizing.

Discovering

Read John 12:1-19.
 Why are the crowds there to welcome Jesus?

To understand where the cry of the people comes from, read Psalm 118:26.

Read Zechariah 9:9-10.
 How does this prophecy correct the political enthusiasm of the crowd?

Explain the Johannine irony in John 12:19. (See Journey 6 for a review of the evangelist's use of irony.)

Exploring Further

Petersen, Norman. *The Gospel of John and the Sociology of Light*. Valley Forge, Pa.: Trinity Press International, 1993.

Rensberger, David. *Johannine Faith and Liberating Community*. Philadelphia: Westminster Press, 1988.

Exploring

People line the road to meet Jesus when he comes to Jerusalem before Passover. They greet him in the traditional way of greeting dignitaries in the Greco-Roman world. He was indeed a warrior king, but one who would wage war on the "world" and celebrate his victorious reign as king from the heights of a cross and finally after his resurrection.

In this Gospel, Jerusalem symbolizes unbelief and rejection by the world, and signals that danger awaits Jesus. With mistaken political expectations, the crowd welcomes Jesus as their king. In ironic prophecy, the Pharisees voice the despair of Caiaphas in John 11:47-48: The "world" has run off after Jesus.

Looking Back

On Journey 7 you made the following discoveries:

- Mary as a faithful and generous disciple stands in contrast to Judas, the unfaithful disciple.
- Hair was a symbol of the whole person, thus a symbol of Mary's total self-gift.
- The anointing of Jesus' feet was, as Jesus stated, a preparation for his burial.
- The great amount of costly nard or perfume was appropriate for a king; Jesus was proclaimed king on his entry into Jerusalem.
- Many people came to believe in Jesus (that is, committed themselves totally to him and his teachings) as a result of the raising of Lazarus. The sign had its proper effect on them.
- The works of the world, ultimately demonstrated in the plan to kill both Jesus and Lazarus, stand in contrast to the goodness of Jesus and his works.
- The passage from Zechariah 9:9-10 serves as a backdrop for understanding the nature of Jesus' kingship.

Journey 8
Reflections on Your Journey

We have now completed what many biblical scholars call the Book of Signs. All of Jesus' miraculous deeds fall within the first twelve chapters of the Gospel, all, that is, except the greatest of all signs—his resurrection. This journey requires that you be alone, so if you are working with a group, each person will do this exercise within his or her own time and space. Making the Gospel a vital part of our lives is of utmost importance. Reflection is one means to advance toward that goal. In this journey, we will utilize a method of reflection that Saint Ignatius Loyola recommended for contemplating the Scriptures. First, read through the entire journey in order to become familiar with the steps. Then proceed with the exercise.

Discovering

1) Find the quietest possible location. Have a pencil and paper at hand. Open your Bible to John 12:1-8. You will need about forty minutes to complete this exercise.

2) Sit in a straight chair, your feet flat on the floor with your hands in your lap and your eyes closed or lowered.

3) Begin to concentrate on your breathing, which will enable your body to relax. Imagine that you are inhaling the light of God's love and peace, and exhaling darkness, fear and anxiety. Continue breathing steadily with a rhythm.

4) Open your eyes and read the story of Mary anointing the feet of Jesus (John 12:1-8).

5) Close your eyes again and imagine yourself in the room as part of the scene—a servant, one of the guests, or one of the disciples. Become familiar with the surroundings by using all your senses: Observe the room, its size and shape; look at the guests, one by one, the expression on each face, what they are wearing and so on; hear the noises in the room, the conversations, the sound of dishes. What is the general mood at the dinner table? (Remember, Lazarus has just been raised from the dead.) Watch Martha as she serves the guests.

6) Focus now on Jesus sitting at the table with Lazarus, his good friend, nearby. Imagine the conversation between the two.

7) Turn your attention now to Mary. In your mind's eye, see her coming into the room with a precious perfume made from an imported herb. Observe every move Mary makes as she stoops to the floor and pours the whole pound of ointment on Jesus' feet. What is the reaction of Jesus, the expression on his face? the reaction of those at table? your own feelings and reaction? Smell the sweet aroma as it fills the room. See her hair as Mary dries Jesus' feet—its color, its fullness, how it looks when she is finished.

8) Now center your attention on Judas. Observe his face, the darkness into which he has entered; hear his murmuring and his objections to "the waste" of the perfume. What are your feelings toward Judas? Hear Jesus' response, his defense of Mary's action. How do you feel when he mentions his burial?

9) Watch Mary as she leaves the room when she is finished. As she passes by you, look into her eyes; see her love, her sorrow.

10) When you have finished, imagine yourself returning to the room and finding Jesus there alone, still with the sweet aroma enveloping him. Sit there with him in the manner with which you feel most comfortable. Look Jesus in the eyes, see his love respond to yours. What do you wish to say to him? Listen to what he is saying to you. Are you comfortable sitting in silence with him as two people often do who love one another?

11) When you have finished your conversation and time with Jesus, take the paper and pen and begin to write any ideas that come to you. You may express them in poetry, prose or even drawings.

Looking Back

On Journey 8 what discoveries did you make?

Journey 9

The Last Supper, Part One— Jesus Washes His Disciples' Feet

Individuals and countries have their own unique ways of showing gratitude, love and devotion to another. I have a friend who sends me funny homemade cards at the most unexpected times. In Latvia, one of the most common demonstrations of love or appreciation is the gift of flowers. Latvians have a saying that if a man on his way home from work has to make a choice between taking his wife flowers or bread, it is advisable to take flowers.

Discovering

This last part of the Gospel of John is frequently designated as the Book of Glory because the Word of God returns to his Father in glory by means of his death and resurrection. Read John 12:20-26. What is Jesus' hour? If necessary, review Journey 2 for its meaning.

In his book *Symbolism in the Fourth Gospel*, Craig Koester states, "All people will lose their selves and their lives—that is a given—but those who lose themselves in service to Christ enter into a relationship that bears fruit and brings them life" (p. 247).

What are some ways that we lose our lives in this sense?

Read John 13:1-20.

What meaning does Jesus give his act of washing the disciples' feet in 13:6-11?

Explain in your own words the paradox of the grain of wheat that must fall into the ground and die in order to bear fruit.

Find another meaning for this symbolic action in 13:12-20.

Exploring

Jesus' washing the feet of his disciples at the Last Supper is another reminder of both the power and the death of Jesus. Even though the Father had given all power to him (John 13:3), he chooses to use that power in an act of menial service and supreme love, an act that the world would consider an act of weakness. A slave might wash another's feet, or even a pupil, out of great devotion, might wash his teacher's feet, but never the reverse.

This act was symbolic of what Jesus would do for his disciples through his death on the cross. The verbs used in 13:4 (laid down; took up) are the same ones Jesus used in 10:17-18 when he spoke of laying down and taking up his life. Thus the evangelist makes the connection between the washing of the feet and Jesus' death on the cross followed by his resurrection.

When Peter protests the footwashing, Jesus insists that Peter could "have no share with" him if Jesus did not wash his feet; in other words, if Jesus does not love and die for him, eternal relationship with him would not be possible. Peter then wants to be washed all over, for he greatly desires that relationship. Jesus indicated, however, that this act of service could not be measured, just as his death was a total act of love that could not be quantified either.

The footwashing was not only a symbol of Jesus' total gift of his life on the cross, but it was also a symbol of the cleansing effect that his death would have on sin. In Johannine theology, sin is a hostile estrangement from God; it is this estrangement that Jesus' death cleanses or washes away.

"[S]ervants are not greater than their master" (13:16); thus Jesus asked his disciples to follow his example and wash one another's feet. Just as Jesus had shown his love for them, they, too, were to show their love for other people, even to the point of total self-sacrifice.

In view of the symbolic meaning of the footwashing, the evangelist's introductory words in 13:1, "Before the feast of Passover...," have special significance. Those words are a reminder that the blood of the Passover lamb had saved the Israelites from physical death at the hand of the angel of death. Jesus replaces the Passover lamb; he sacrifices his life for the sins of the people so that they might be rescued from eternal death.

Discovering

Read John 13:21-30.

What comparison or contrast does this passage present to the previous one?

What might the evangelist have meant by the statement, "And it was night" (13:30)?

Recall the theme of light and darkness in this Gospel. What is its significance? (If you need to review these concepts, turn to Journeys 1 and 3 for help.)

Exploring

Jesus' act of love, symbolized by the footwashing, stands in stark contrast to the prediction of Judas' betrayal of love and intimate fellowship in John 13:21-20. The evangelist forewarned in 13:2: "The devil had already put it into the heart of Judas son of Iscariot to betray him."

And now the foreboding becomes a reality: "Satan entered into him" (13:27), that is, he became the agent of Satan, who embodies sin, death and all evil. The fallen disciple will act in unison with the powers of darkness.

Reclining was part of long dinners, such as the Passover meal, in Palestine in the first century. The gesture of handing a bit of bread to Judas was a sign of affection toward a friend with whom one dined. It was also reminiscent of dipping the bitter herbs into the *haroseth* sauce at the Passover meal. Jesus was inviting him to think about what he was about to do. Judas did not respond in love, but having accepted the morsel, he departed and plunged himself into darkness. Jesus had declared earlier (8:12), "I am the light of the world. Whoever follows me will never walk in darkness but will have the light of life." Judas has chosen not to follow the light, but rather to walk in the darkness.

The indication of Judas as the betrayer gives us our first introduction to "the one whom Jesus loved" (13:23), or the Beloved Disciple. Tradition attributes to this personage the authority behind the Johannine Gospel. He was probably an eyewitness and follower of Jesus while he was on earth. He is never named in the Gospel, probably because the evangelist wants the reader to see in "the disciple whom Jesus loved" the ideal model for Christian behavior and relationship to Jesus.

Discovering

Read John 13:31-38.

What is the glory of which Jesus speaks in John 13:31-32?

Write down the lines that have particular significance for you.

Read Leviticus 19:18.

How does this command compare with Jesus' command in 13:34?

What is the greatest challenge this command poses for you?

Write a short prayer asking for the grace to live the command to love one another as Jesus would have us live it.

Exploring

Even though there was the command to love one another in the Old Testament (Leviticus 19:8), the radical dimension of Jesus' command to love one another made it distinct in that we are to love as Jesus loved. His love was indeed radical because he loved us even to the point of laying down his life, an act designated by Jesus as the greatest act of love: "No one has greater love than this, to lay down one's life for one's friends" (15:13).

Peter boldly declares that he has that kind of love for

Jesus; he will follow his Lord no matter what the consequences, even if it means that he dies with him. Jesus' prediction of Peter's threefold denial stands as an example of human intent in contrast to actual behavior. Peter will indeed "lay down" his life for Jesus as Jesus will inform Peter later (21:18). However, it will not be before Peter has denied three times that he is a disciple of Jesus.

Looking Back

On Journey 9 you made the following discoveries:

- We call chapters 13—21 in John's Gospel the Book of Glory because it was through Jesus' death and resurrection that he was glorified.
- The footwashing was symbolic of Jesus' greatest act of self-giving on the cross as well as a symbol of the effect his death would have on human estrangement from God.
- Sin in Johannine theology is estrangement in one's relationship with God.
- Judas' entrance into the night symbolized his choice to reject the light and embrace the darkness of Satan.
- When Jesus handed Judas the morsel, it was an act of friendship.
- What makes Jesus' command to love "new" is that he asks his followers to love *as he has loved us*, which was to give his life for us.

Exploring Further

Eller, Vernard. *The Beloved Disciple: His Name, His Story, His Thought*. Grand Rapids, Mich.: Wm. B. Eerdmans, 1987.

Koester, Craig R. *Symbolism in the Fourth Gospel: Meaning, Mystery, Community*. Minneapolis: Fortress Press, 1995.

Journey 10

Jesus Prepares His Disciples for His Departure

When my mother was near death, she told me something that touched me deeply. She said that she really didn't mind dying because that meant she would be with God, my father and her children who had died at birth. But, on the other hand, it meant she had to leave the rest of her children here on earth. It made me think of Jesus' farewell to his disciples the night before his death. Even though Jesus is going to his glorification with the Father, there is a note of pathos in chapters 14 through 17; Jesus empathizes with his disciples in their sorrow that he is about to leave them.

Discovering

Read John 14:1-31.

Think about a time in your life in which faith alone seemed to get you through a difficulty. Write about your experience in the space below.

What do you think Jesus means by the many mansions in his Father's house?

Write a short prayer asking for something in Jesus' name that will promote the works of Jesus on earth.

Exploring

Jesus addressed these words to his followers to help them understand that his leaving them through death and resurrection would be to their advantage. Their sorrow will turn to joy.

Jesus speaks of "mansions" in his Father's house, a metaphor for heaven or the dwelling place of God. The first-century philosopher Philo spoke of heaven as "the paternal house," a metaphor, most likely, for the dwelling of God. Jesus promises to prepare a heavenly home for them; later he will return to take them there. When Thomas objects that they do not know the way, Jesus explains that he himself is the way, the only avenue to salvation and thus to the Father. Whoever knows Jesus and sees him, knows and sees the Father.

Jesus puts emphasis on the role of "belief"—that is, the need to totally trust him and all that he says. Only through such belief will they be able to look beyond the cross to the resurrection. That kind of belief in Jesus will enable them to perform the same works that Jesus performed in his ministry. To ask in Jesus' name is to ask Jesus, because Jesus and the Father are one.

Discovering

Read John 14:26 to 16:15.

John uses the Greek word *paraclete* for "Holy Spirit." In the Bible that you are using, what is the translation for the Holy Spirit in these passages?

Look in another Bible, a different translation, and see how Paraclete is translated. Read the following verses and write what the Holy Spirit Paraclete is to do for Jesus' followers. The variety of translations for the Spirit Paraclete reflects translators' efforts to show in the translation the different roles of the Paraclete.

John 14:16-17

John 14:26

John 15:26

John 16:7-11

John 16:12-15

Exploring

In John 14:16, Jesus seems to indicate that he himself was a Paraclete during his earthly ministry because he speaks of another Paraclete. In the following verse, he identifies the Paraclete that is yet to come as "the spirit of Truth." But the Paraclete that is yet to come is different from Jesus the Paraclete, because Jesus' followers will not be able to see the Spirit Paraclete.

The Spirit Paraclete will act as a counsellor who upholds the cause of a disciple in his or her trials with the world, when the world stands in opposition to following Christ (14:16-17). He will also clarify for the follower what Jesus has already taught, disclosing the implication of Jesus' words and deeds for his disciples in the world (14:26; 16:12-15). The Spirit Paraclete will act on behalf of the disciples of Jesus as a prosecuting attorney would, that is, the Paraclete will go on the offensive against Satan and evil in the world (16:7-11). (You may wish to check your answers with mine.) Therefore, it is understandable why Jesus spoke of "another Paraclete" as if he himself were a Paraclete—what the Spirit Paraclete will do for the disciples is that which Jesus did when he was with them.

The peace that Jesus promises his disciples (14:27) is much more than tranquility. The Greek word for peace (*eirene*) conveys the notion of wholeness of personhood which, in the Gospel of John, is the gift of salvation. What he promises then is to fulfill his mission on the cross as the Word made flesh.

Discovering

Read John 16:16-33.
　What is the hour of which Jesus speaks in 16:25?

Exploring

The sorrow that fills the disciples' hearts as Jesus speaks of his departure from this world is compared by Jesus to birth pangs. They last but a time, and then the sufferings are turned to joy when Jesus conquers sin and death in his resurrection. Their joy, however, is two-pronged; it is also the joy of the Spirit, accompanied by sorrow in persecution by the world.

　Our union with Christ in the Spirit will be an intimate relationship with the Father as well, since Jesus and the Father are one, and we are one in him. Therefore, whatever his disciples ask of him in Jesus' name will be Jesus' prayer as well.

Looking Back

On Journey 10 you made the following discoveries:

- *Paraclete* is the Johannine term for Holy Spirit; it conveys the notion that the Spirit Jesus promised is to be to his disciples a counselor, a consoler, a teacher and their defense against Satan.
- The peace that Jesus promises his disciples is the gift of salvation.

Exploring Further

Comblin, Jose. *Sent From the Father: Meditations on the Fourth Gospel*. Maryknoll, N.Y.: Orbis Books, 1979.

Servotte, Herman. *According to John*. London: Darton, Longman, & Todd, 1992/94.

Journey 11
'I Am the Vine; You Are the Branches'

When one walks the streets and roads of Jerusalem, Jericho and Galilee, one sees vineyard after vineyard. Most are well kept. In the fall or winter, a vinedresser cuts away the dead branches from the stock of the grapevine, stacks them in ghastly bunches and then takes them away for disposal. When spring comes, the vinedresser is back again cutting away small useless growth that would sap the strength from the more healthy vines.

In the last journey, you studied about the intimate relationship that Jesus wished to maintain with his disciples even after he had left them to return to the Father. In this journey, Jesus describes our union with him in another way.

In the allegory of the vine and the branches, Jesus graphically portrays his intimacy with us. He was familiar with vineyards in Palestine and the work that was required to keep them bearing good fruit. He must have watched the pruning process many times as he walked from place to place in his country.

Discovering

Read John 15:1-26.

An allegory is a comparison in which each character or object in the story corresponds to a deeper reality. In the space provided, write the corresponding reality (that is, who or what the symbols represent) to the following word or words from the allegory of the vine and the branches in John 15:1-26.

the true vine

the vinedresser

the branches

the fruit

Read Isaiah 5:1-7. Read Jeremiah 2:21. Read Psalm 80:8-13. In these passages from the Old Testament, who or what is represented by the vine?

Describe the condition of the vine.

Set aside about fifteen or twenty minutes or more for the following exercise.

1) Find a quiet place and sit comfortably with your eyes closed, breathing in and out rhythmically.

2) Think of yourself as united with Jesus as intimately as a branch is united to a tree. Enjoy this intimacy and thank Jesus for it before moving to the next step.

3) Now, with the graced awareness you have in regard to the intimate relationship you enjoy with the risen Lord, see the divine vinedresser standing before you ready to prune away anything that keeps you from being even more intimate in your relationship with the Lord. What does he wish to say to you? Remember that your union with Jesus can enable you and even inspire you to let go of any dead branches.

4) In the space below, name the graces that you have received in this time of recognition of your union with Jesus.

Then write a short prayer of thanksgiving for these graces.

Exploring

Beginning in the Maccabean era in the second century B.C., there was widespread use of the vine on Jewish coins. Josephus, the renowned Jewish historian who was conscripted to write Jewish history for the Romans, wrote that Herod had a golden vine placed at the entrance of the temple he built (*Antiquities*, 15.395). For centuries, the vine or vineyard had been a symbol of Israel in the Hebrew writings. In all its applications to Israel, the vine, or vineyard, portrays the nation in its infidelity to God and lack of fruitfulness in its mission as God's people. For example, "...I planted you as a choice vine,/from the purest stock./How then did you turn degenerate/and become a wild vine?" (Jeremiah 2:21).

Israel was subject to God's judgment because it lacked fruit. Why then would Jesus, who was indeed faithful to the Father in every aspect of his life, be presented as a vine? It was probably meant to have more than one significance. First, the image of the vine highlights the contrast between Jesus' fidelity to the Father and Israel's infidelity to God. For that reason, Jesus is the true and faithful vine. Second, the vine also acknowledges the difference between Jesus as the vine and the Father as the vinedresser, while at the same time, it conveys the notion of their unity—the vine and the branches are the same entity. Thirdly, the image is carried further; Jesus is the vine and his disciples are the branches. The symbol then denotes the intimate relationship Jesus has with his followers.

Discovering

Read John 6:51-58. Read John 15:7-17 again.
    What sacramental theme may be represented by the vine? Explain.

Exploring

Since the allegory of the vine and the branches is placed within the Last Supper scene, in which John has no institution of the Eucharist, probably the evangelist meant for us to see in the vine another symbol—that of the Eucharist. The vine easily reminds one of the eucharistic cup, especially since in Mark 14:25 and Matthew 26:29, the phrase "the fruit of the vine" designates the contents of the cup in the institution of the Eucharist.

In *The Didache* (pronounced "DID-a-kay," a Greek word that means "teaching"), an early Christian manual on morals and church order, the following words occur in the eucharistic blessing: "We thank [*eucharistein*, the Greek word for "giving thanks" from which we derive our English word *Eucharist*] you, our Father, for the holy vine of David your servant, which you revealed to us through Jesus your servant." John has similar words in his account of the multiplication of the loaves in 6:11 (see Journey 4 on the eucharistic theme). Certainly, the theme of intimate union that runs throughout John 15—17 would suggest that the vine and the branches evoke thoughts of the intimate union with Jesus which we have in the Eucharist.

Discovering

Read 1 Corinthians 12:12-17.
    What similarities do you find between the image used in Paul's letter to the Corinthians and the vine?

Exploring

How does one bear or not bear fruit? In the Gospel of John, faith is a personal commitment to Jesus and his teachings. A commitment to Jesus' teachings entails keeping his commands, especially the command to love one another. One who lives such a life of faith in an intimate relationship with Jesus has life; in other words, he or she carries on the works of Jesus and thus bears fruit. Not to accept the invitation to be one with Jesus is to refuse his life, and without his life, one cannot bear fruit for the Kingdom of God. In John's dualistic way of expression, there is no in-between stage; either one bears fruit or not.

Jesus speaks of trimming away the branches that prevent fruitfulness. His disciples, however, do not need to be "trimmed clean," for they love and thus are fruit-bearing branches (15:23). They will remain clean by remaining in intimate union with Jesus by reason of his death and resurrection. He will remain in them so that they may continue bearing fruit in service to others. His life in his disciples enables them to bear fruit and thus give glory to the Father (15:7-8). This union with Jesus gives the disciples joy, which results in fruit-bearing, that is, love and service to others (15:12). From the viewpoint of service, the disciple is a servant; but from the perspective of Jesus' love, the disciple is Jesus' "beloved" (15:15).

Discovering

Read John 17:1-26.

For whom is Jesus praying?

Summarize the various things Jesus prays for:

What connection do you see between the allegory of the vine and the branches and this prayer of Jesus?

Exploring

Rarely in this Gospel does John tell us specifically that Jesus prays, whereas in the other Gospels, especially in Luke's, there are many references to Jesus praying and even going off alone to pray. As the supper scene in the Gospel of John draws to an end, however, Jesus prays a most sublime and poetic prayer for his disciples—those who were at table with him and all future followers as well. Saint Cyril of Alexandria saw in this prayer Jesus' high priestly intercession for the people. No longer do his followers need an earthly high priest to intercede for them; they have the perfect intercessor who is returning to the Father in glory.

This prayer of Jesus on the eve of his death revolves around three themes or principle concerns of Jesus before his passion: (1) His earthly mission gives way now to his glorification with the Father (17:1-5); (2) he wishes his disciples to be a community of faith and love when he is no longer with them (17:6-19); (3) he desires that future generations also be united in love (17:20-26).

The hour has come for Jesus to lay down his life out of love for his friends, so that they may "know" the Father. To "know" the Father, according to the fourth evangelist, is eternal life (17:3). The Semitic sense of "to know" implies intimate union. Jesus has protected his followers, and they belong to the Father. Jesus prays for their further protection and dedication to his work of making the Father known (17:9-19). He also prays for the unity of future followers of his way (17:20-26).

Discovering

You will need about fifteen minutes for the following exercise:

1) Sit quietly with your eyes closed and breathe deeply for a few seconds.

2) Be aware of Jesus' intimate union with you, a union as close as that of a branch to the stock of the vine.

3) Think of another image aside from the one Jesus used which expresses that union in a meaningful way for you.

4) Ponder his love for you in the Sacrament of the Eucharist.

5) Thank Jesus for your intimate relationship with him, and ask him to increase your awareness of it.

Looking Back

On Journey 11 you made the following discoveries:

- In an allegory, such as the vine and the branches, each person or thing corresponds to another reality.
- The allegory of the vine and the branches is a striking reminder of our intimate union with the risen Lord and the Father's love in "trimming away" anything that impedes that union with Jesus.
- In the Old Testament, a vine or vineyard is frequently used as a symbol of unfaithful Israel, subject to the judgment of God.
- Jesus is the true vine because, unlike Israel, he was faithful in his mission to God's people.
- Bearing fruit entails remaining in Jesus and he in us; only in that relationship of intimate union can we bear fruit through our love and service of others.
- *The Didache* is an early Christian writing in which is found a reference to the vine in relation to the Eucharist.
- In Jesus' prayer for the disciples at the Last Supper, we are reminded of Jesus' love for us as demonstrated in the symbols of both the good shepherd and the vine and the branches.

Exploring Further

Countryman, William. *The Mystical Way in the Fourth Gospel*. Revised edition. Valley Forge, Pa.: Trinity Press, 1994.

Hanson, Richard Simon. *Journey to Resurrection*. Mahwah, N.J.: Paulist Press, 1986.

Journey 12
The Garden and a Challenge to Discipleship

Having read the Gospel of John up to this point, you are well aware of the tremendous differences that exist between the Fourth Gospel and the other three. You have noted John's emphasis on Jesus' divinity while maintaining his humanity. Jesus who speaks with no reservations about coming down from the Father, being one with the Father and laying down his life of his own accord is the same Jesus who weeps at the tomb of Lazarus and empathizes with the grief of his disciples at the Last Supper.

John must have had available to him one or more accounts of the passion narrative, such as the Synoptic Gospels. As with the rest of the Gospel, however, his perspective and style differ from that of the other evangelists; his theological and historical reasons for writing a Gospel are distinct; and he has some traditions to which the other evangelists did not have access. The parts of the passion narrative that are similar to those of the other Gospels reflect a tradition in the early Church that was already widely accepted before John's writing. The sections that differ not only indicate a separate tradition, but also reflect a distinct theology and style of expression.

As we enter into the passion narrative proper, you will find that John's christological emphasis has not changed. The Word of God who became flesh and lived among us as the light of the world now encounters, for a final showdown, the world of darkness and disbelief at the height of its power.

Discovering

Read John 18:1-12.

Compare this passage with Mark 14:32-50 and write in the space below the differing aspects that you discovered.

What possible reasons can you think of that would account for the differences?

Exploring

One of the major differences one finds in comparing the garden scene in John's account with the same in the Synoptic accounts is that there is no agony in the garden in the Fourth Gospel. Already in John 12:27, Jesus has prayed: "Now my soul is troubled. And what should I say—'Father, save me from this hour?' No, it is for this reason that I have come to this hour." Therefore, John can omit the agony from the garden scene and put emphasis on the fact that Jesus "lays down" his life and that no one takes it from him. His will is the will of the Father who sent him in order that the world might have life.

In accordance with the prescriptions of Passover to remain within the confines of the city, Jesus and his disciples go to a familiar place after celebrating the Passover meal. Only in John is there mention of a cohort of soldiers (six hundred Roman soldiers) in addition to temple police who went there to arrest Jesus. Certainly, the Romans always stationed troops in Jerusalem during festivals to keep order. But strange as it seems, both Jewish forces (the temple police) and Gentile forces (the cohort) join in strength against the good shepherd who is light of the world and who came to earth only to do his Father's will.

Judas, a fallen disciple, in embracing the darkness, has joined the violent forces of Rome and the anger of the Jewish authorities against Jesus. Under his leadership, they come bearing lanterns, torches and weapons. What effect can the mere artificial light of lanterns and torches have for those who reject the true light?

Discovering

Read Psalm 27:2. Read Ezekiel 1:28; 3:23; 44:4. Read Daniel 10:7-9. How do these passages help the evangelist express the identity of the One whom the soldiers come to arrest?

Read John 18:13-14, 19-24.

Exploring

John omits the kiss by Judas, for he wishes to underscore the fact that Jesus is in charge of his own destiny. Jesus lays down his life willingly and of his own accord (10:17-18).

The evangelist states that Jesus knows what is to take place (18:4). With great drama John unfolds the confrontation of light with darkness. Jesus boldly and without fear takes the initiative in addressing the arresting party: "Whom are you looking for?" It seems as though Jesus initiates his own arrest.

When they respond that they are looking for Jesus of Nazareth, this man with a common name from a lowly village startles them by answering with the divine "I AM" (18:5, 8; usually translated into English as "I am he"), words that identify him as the revelation of God.

The stunning reaction of the soldiers is one that is common when human beings encounter the presence of God; the forces of darkness fall to the ground in utter helplessness before the light of the world. After a second inquiry and response, Jesus answers as the good shepherd concerned for his sheep: "Let these men go" (18:8).

To defend Jesus from the fate of the cross he has

chosen to embrace, Peter strikes out by cutting off the ear of one of the arresting party. Only minutes later, he will deny his discipleship with Jesus. Jesus' reference to the cup of suffering indicates his obedient acceptance of his Father's will, and he rejects Peter's would-be protection.

John alone reports that Jesus was then taken to Annas. Annas held a patriarchal position among the Jewish leaders. He had been high priest from A.D. 6 to 15, but his deposition by Pilate's predecessor did not diminish respect for him among the Jewish leaders. Five of his sons, a grandson and a son-in-law held the office of high priest after him, and they were notorious for their corruption and greed. Before this ungodly man stands the Son of God who is questioned about his teachings. Jesus responds with the truth and is slapped in return.

Discovering

Read John 18:15-18, 25-27.
Write the dialogue between Peter and his inquisitors:

The Maid:

Peter:

"They" (probably refers to the servants and the guards):

Peter:

One of the slaves of the high priest:

Peter:

What is Peter actually denying?

Exploring

"The other disciple" who got permission from the gatekeeper for Peter to enter is identified in John 20:2 as "the disciple whom Jesus loved."

By placing the story of Peter's denials before and after the account of Jesus' interrogation before Annas, the evangelist is able to contrast fidelity and infidelity. The fearlessness and fidelity to the truth on the part of Jesus stand in stark contrast to the cowardice and lies of Peter. At the moment when Peter is called to witness to his identification with Jesus, he fails miserably three

times. The cock sounds its affirmation of Jesus' prediction; there are no tears of sorrow as in the Synoptic Gospels. Peter's reinstatement to discipleship will come later in John 21.

Discovering

Peter's denials of association with Jesus stand as warnings to all who would be followers of Jesus. Read again John 18:15-18, 25-27.

You will need about twenty minutes for the following prayer exercise:

1) With your Bible on your lap, sit with this passage in front of you.

2) Close your eyes and relax. Empty your mind of all outside distractions.

3) Now put yourself in Peter's place and take his lines in the story. Of what is he afraid? What would you be afraid of in that situation?

4) Speak to Jesus in your heart about any fears you may have in regard to being his witness in your daily life.

5) Write below the fears you have in witnessing to your identity as a Christian, a follower of Jesus who is called to live as Jesus taught. What do you think is the basis of your fears?

Looking Back

On Journey 12 you made the following discoveries:

- The garden to which Jesus went with his disciples would have been within the confines of Jerusalem in accord with Passover prescriptions.
- In John's account of the garden scene, there is no agony. Already in John 12:17, Jesus has prayed to his Father about accepting his hour of sufferings.
- John continues in the passion narrative his presentation of Jesus as "I AM," a designation of divinity that Jesus appropriates for himself in the Gospel of John.

- The powers of darkness are embodied in Judas and in the Jewish authorities who are in opposition to Jesus.
- In the trial before Annas, a former high priest of ongoing prestige among the Jewish authorities, Jesus' courageous truth and witness to his deeds stand against the lies and cowardice of Peter.
- Peter's denials in the Fourth Gospel are denials of his discipleship, and they endure as a warning to all who carry the title "Christian."

Exploring Further

Brown, Raymond E. *The Death of the Messiah: A Commentary on the Passion Narratives in the Four Gospels*. New York: Doubleday, 1993.

Stanley, David. *Jesus in Gethsemani: The Early Church Reflects on the Sufferings of Jesus*. New York: Paulist Press, 1980.

Journey 13
Jesus and Pilate

In the trial before Pilate, we see Johannine theology and literary skill at its peak. Many themes introduced earlier in the Gospel will come to full play in this part of the passion story. Jesus will witness to ultimate truth while truth is perverted by his enemies. Light and darkness will be counterposed. Irony will be used to unmask the hypocrisy of Jesus' enemies and Pilate's lack of understanding of Jesus' identity. One gets the impression that Pilate is as much on trial as is Jesus.

John sets up this trial in seven scenes, situating them alternately between the inside and the outside, a literary technique that heightens the interest of the reader and at the same time highlights the contrast between light and darkness.

The trial before Pilate is a classic illustration of how the evangelist has reshaped, for theological reasons and dramatic presentation, the traditions he had preserved.

Discovering

Read John 18:28—19:16.

There are two settings for the trial before Pilate: one is on the outside of the praetorium with the enemies of Jesus; the other is inside with Jesus. In the spaces below, indicate the seven scenes by verses and the persons "on stage" in each scene.

• SCENE 1 (Outside)

Verses:

PERSONS IN SCENE:

• SCENE 2 (Inside)

Verses:

PERSONS IN SCENE:

• SCENE 3 (Outside)

Verses:

PERSONS IN SCENE:

• SCENE 4 (Inside)

Verses:

PERSONS IN SCENE:

• SCENE 5 (Outside)

Verses:

PERSONS IN SCENE:

• SCENE 6 (Inside)

Verses:

PERSONS IN SCENE:

• SCENE 7 (Outside)

Verses:

PERSONS IN SCENE:

Exploring

With a note of irony, John states that the Jewish leaders did not enter the praetorium so as not to defile themselves; otherwise, they would have been prevented from celebrating the Passover. According to Jewish thought, the dwellings of Gentiles were unclean. Ironically, the religious leaders are worried about physical defilement, while at the same time they are willing to put an innocent person to death.

More than any of the evangelists, John makes it clear why the people brought Jesus to Pilate—only a Roman court could hand down an order to execute a person. Jesus' enemies have in mind a civil offense; they present Jesus as a revolutionary with pretentions to the imperial throne. They have turned their backs on the light of the world and now they want to extinguish the light.

Discovering

Read John 18:28—19:16 again.

How many times are the following words and phrases used?

King of the Jews:

king:

kingdom:

How many times does Pilate declare that Jesus is not guilty?

Exploring

Going inside, Pilate questions Jesus about a political charge that is implied by the fact that Jesus was handed over to him for capital punishment. "Are you the King of the Jews?" (18:33).

Jesus' kingship is a major theme in the passion narrative. "The King of the Jews" is used six times, "king" is used five times, "kingdom" appears three times, Jesus is mocked as a king, and he is crowned with thorns and clothed with a purple cloak (a symbol of royalty) at the time of his scourging.

In a previous Passover, the crowd had wanted to make Jesus a king, but he hid himself from them (6:14-15). Again, when he entered Jerusalem for this Passover, they had hailed their king (12:13-15), whereupon Jesus found a donkey and sat upon it. Always in this Gospel, before the passion narrative, the understanding of the people concerning his messiahship or kingship was clouded by political hopes. Now Jesus is

willing to accept the title of king (18:37); his helpless condition verified that his was not an earthly kingdom. He was a king whose most sovereign action would be to die on a cross for the salvation of all people.

Discovering

Read John 19:1-3. Read 1 Maccabees 10:20, 57-65; 11:57-58.

What are you to understand by the mocking of Jesus in the purple cloak and the crown of thorns?

Exploring

In Jewish literature of both the Old and New Testaments, the center passage in a series of parallel ones is the part that calls for the reader's attention. The center scene of the seven making up the trial before Pilate is the scourging in which Jesus is mockingly crowned with thorns and clothed in purple, the color used for royalty. Using his skill at irony again, John shows us in the scourging scene that when Jesus is least suspected of being a king, symbols of kingship are unwittingly thrust upon him. What his persecutors do not understand is that Jesus' kingdom is the kingdom of truth, the truth about God's sovereignty, the acceptance of which guarantees salvation to all who would embrace it.

Discovering

Read John 19:5-16. Read Exodus 12:1-13.

How does the passage from Exodus enlighten one's understanding of John 19:5-16?

Exploring

After repeated attempts to save Jesus, Pilate makes one last try. He brings Jesus (still wearing the purple robe of mockery) outside and presents him to the people. Instead of being shocked by the pitiable sight, they call out all the more for his death by crucifixion (19:13-16).

The imperial governor of Rome takes his place upon the judgment seat as the people still clamor for the death of Jesus. There is ambiguity in the Greek verb denoting "sat upon" (19:13). Even though it was in reality the Roman governor who sat upon the place of judgment, John cleverly left it ambiguous so that, grammatically and theologically speaking, it could have been Jesus who sat upon the place of judgment. This is probably John's way of asking the reader to contemplate, "Just who is on trial? Is it Jesus? Or is it Pilate, who embodies the world?"

John cleverly notes, "It was the preparation day for Passover, and it was about noon" (19:14). It is easy to miss the last phrase, "it was about noon," but it is important. At noon on the preparation day for Passover, the priests in the Temple began to slaughter the Passover lambs. The Passover festival had begun. Passover was the celebration of God's deliverance of the Israelites from Egyptian slavery; now a new Passover was about to occur in which God, in Jesus, accomplishes the salvation of all nations. The Passover lamb would no longer be the supreme expression of God's salvation; Jesus, the Lamb of God, will replace the Passover lamb and free humanity from slavery to sin.

Pilate, after having declared Jesus innocent several times, now offers the people their King. A nation that had always maintained that their king was God and all earthly kings his representatives, now rejects the only real king and chooses a foreign king who has no rights over them: "We have no king but the emperor" (19:15c). And Pilate hands Jesus over to them for crucifixion.

Discovering

Sit silently with your eyes closed in the presence of the scourged Lord. Speak to him in the silence of your heart.

Looking Back

On Journey 13 you made the following discoveries:

- John uses his literary skills to present theological themes such as witness, kingship, Jesus as Passover victim and so on in Jesus' trial before Pilate.

- The trial scene illustrates the encounter of darkness and light; one who chooses the darkness in preference to the light stands as one condemned before the judgment seat of the king of kings.
- The kingship of Jesus is emphasized in the trial scene in order to accentuate the theological notion that, in his death, Jesus gained sovereignty over Satan and darkness and reigns as King over all peoples.
- It is important to remember that John's expression "the Jews" refers to the enemies of Jesus and not to the Jewish people.

Exploring Further

La Potterie, Ignace de. *The Hour of Jesus*. New York: Alba House, 1983.

Senior, Donald. *The Passion of Jesus in the Gospel of John*. Collegeville, Minn.: Michael Glazier/The Liturgical Press, 1991.

Journey 14
The Crucifixion, Death and Burial

John's account of Jesus' crucifixion, death and burial differs in many details and in its theology from that of the Synoptic Gospels. The fourth evangelist has reinterpreted common elements from tradition, but he also adds incidents that do not appear in the other Gospels.

In the Gospel of John, the motif that dominated the trial, namely, the kingship of Jesus, is carried through in these scenes as well, especially in the controversy over the inscription on the cross. Jesus maintains a composure that is reminiscent of one who is king, and the cross itself becomes the enthronement of Jesus as he holds his destiny in his own hands. Jesus ends his divine mission with a decisive, "It is finished" (19:30).

Missing from the Fourth Gospel are the mockery of the crowds, the darkness over the whole earth, Jesus' prayer for his enemies, the conversation with one of those crucified with him, the cry of desolation, the rending of the Temple veil and the centurion's confession of Jesus as the Son of God—all found in one or more of the Synoptic Gospels.

The insights of the early Church into the significance of Jesus' death as his hour of glory and exaltation is more clearly reflected in this Gospel than in the other three. One of the subtle reminders that the cross is Jesus' throne of exaltation is the fact that after the scourging and mocking of Jesus in the other Gospels, explicit mention is made that they removed the purple cloak from Jesus. In this Gospel, removal of the purple robe is never mentioned. It is John's skillful way of adding to the theme of Jesus' reign from the cross.

Discovering

Read John 19:16-22.
   Compare John 19:17 with Mark 15:21. How do you account for the difference?

Compare John 19:19-22 with Mark 1:26. Why do you think this incident is amplified in the Gospel of John?

Exploring

When the evangelist describes the inscription, his use of irony helps to highlight the kingship of Jesus. The highest worldly authority present at the scene proclaims and puts in writing, "Jesus of Nazareth, the King of the Jews" (19:19). When his adversaries object to its wording, Pilate refuses to change it. He writes it in Hebrew for the Jews' understanding, in Latin so that the Romans would know it, and in Greek (the universal language of the day) that all nations might understand it. Thus Pilate unwittingly proclaims Jesus' kingship over all peoples. The acronym INRI, commonly seen over Jesus' head in depictions of the crucifixion, comes from the Latin version, *Iesus Nazarenus Rex Iudeorum*.

Discovering

Read John 19:23-30.
   How do each of the Old Testament passages below help interpret Jesus' passion and death?

Read Deuteronomy 21:22-23.

Read Psalms 22:19 and 34:30.

Read Exodus 12:46.

Read Zechariah 12:10.

Exploring

According to custom, the executioners divided Jesus' clothing among themselves. The tunic, however, was made of one piece of cloth, so they cast lots for it (19:24). The meaning of the seamless cloth left intact is unclear. Some scholars maintain that the seamless garment represents the unity of the Church for which Jesus prayed at the Last Supper. Others, however, think that it signifies Jesus' priestly role on the cross, in which case, Jesus would be seen as both priest and victim who replaces the priesthood and victims of the old law.

The two important characters who are never named in this Gospel, "his mother" and "the disciple whom he loved," both stand at the cross. "The disciple whom he loved" is not only the historical link of the Johannine community with the earthly Jesus, but he is also symbolic and thus left unnamed so as to be a model for all future disciples. He was an intimate friend of Jesus and he never forsook him throughout all his trials. "His mother" is also unnamed in this Gospel so that all followers of Jesus might see in her their mother, and thus perceive their own relationship with Jesus as that of a brother or sister. Already at the foot of the cross stand a small community of believers.

John (19:28-29) saw in Jesus' thirst and the sour wine given to him a fulfillment of Psalm 69:21: "...for my thirst they gave me vinegar to drink." Jesus' last words, "It is finished," conclude his sufferings and death and indicate that they are the crowning point of his mission on earth and his obedience to the Father.

Death of a crucified person sometimes came only after days on the cross. But according to Jewish law (Deuteronomy 21:22-23), bodies could not hang on the cross overnight. Thus battering the legs was frequently the way in which death was brought on more quickly. The writer, however, noted that they did not break Jesus' legs since he was already dead, thus fulfilling Psalm 34:30 and Exodus 12:46 and indicating Jesus as the Passover lamb.

However, one of the soldiers did pierce Jesus' side, from which came forth blood and water. Blood signified his humanity and the water, his Spirit, which would remain with his followers. In John 7:37-39, Jesus contended that "living water" (the Spirit) would flow out of him. When seen in light of Jesus' breathing the Spirit upon the disciples on Easter evening, we can say that the gift of the Spirit is the gift of the whole paschal mystery.

Discovering

Read John 19:38-42.

Where did you encounter Nicodemus before in this study of John's Gospel?

Exploring

The comment that Joseph of Arimathea was, through fear, a secret disciple of Jesus and that Nicodemus had come to Jesus by night probably reflects the situation of many Jewish believers of John's day. Thus the Gospel stands as a challenge to them to witness openly concerning the identity of Jesus as their Lord and King. Joseph of Arimathea and Nicodemus are reminders that it is never too late.

The myrrh and aloes were used for burial to quench the odor of decay; they may represent an inadequate faith in Jesus' resurrection on the part of these two men. The amount of myrrh that was brought, about a hundred pounds, would have been suitable only for a king and is meant to highlight again the kingship of Jesus.

Joseph of Arimathea and Nicodemus laid Jesus in a new tomb in a garden instead of a common criminal's grave (19:41). Both the tomb and the garden are highly symbolic. The new tomb is appropriate for the Son of God who finished his earthly career as the messiah/king of all nations. The garden speaks of royalty, for in the Old Testament, tombs of kings were frequently located in gardens (see 2 Kings 21:18, 26) as was the tomb of King David (Neh 3:16).

Looking Back

On Journey 14 you made the following discoveries:

- The crucifixion, death and burial of Jesus in the Fourth Gospel carry through with the theme of Jesus' kingship.
- Jesus' crucifixion is his enthronement and glorification.
- The inscription highlights the kingship of Jesus over all nations.
- INRI, which appears above Jesus' head in depictions of the crucifixion, is an acronym for the Latin translation of the inscription.
- The seamless garment that remains undivided may represent the unity of the Church for which Jesus prayed at the Last Supper.
- The unnamed disciple is a model for all believers, and the unnamed mother of Jesus is a reminder of the Christian's relationship as brother or sister to Jesus.
- Many aspects of Jesus' death are understood in light of Old Testament Scriptures.
- The hundred pounds of spices used for Jesus' burial underscores the theme of kingship as does the new tomb and the garden.

Exploring Further

Brown, Raymond E., Karl Dunfried, Joseph Fitzmyer and John Rheumann, editors. *Mary in the New Testament*. Philadelphia: Fortress Press, 1978.

Heil, John P. *Blood and Water: The Death and Resurrection of Jesus in John 18-21*. Washington, D.C.: The Catholic Biblical Association of America, 1995.

Hengel, Martin. *Crucifixion*. Translated by John Bowden. Philadelphia: Fortress Press, 1977.

Journey 15

The Risen Lord Appears in Jerusalem

We live in an age in which we don't have to wait long for many things—we have e-mail, the Internet, FAX machines, instant hot cereal, microwave ovens and so on.

The Easter Vigil liturgy, however, reminds Christians that not everything is instant. We must still await the second coming of the Lord in glory. The early Christians celebrated the Easter Vigil in anticipation of the second coming of Christ. It was an all-night vigil during which they prayed and read from the Scriptures. Only at dawn was the Mass celebrated and the catechumens baptized.

Today, we celebrate the vigil with the lighting of the new fire. We watch the tiny light in the darkness; suddenly the whole church is filled with small candle lights whose flames come from the paschal candle, a symbol of Jesus Christ, the light of the world. In the Blessing of the Fire, the priest prays that God will "bring us one day to the feast of eternal light." Thus every Holy Saturday we carry on in a most solemn celebration the tradition of waiting for the second coming as did the early Church.

Discovering

Read John 20:1-10.

In your own words, describe the empty tomb scene.

Take about twenty minutes to sit alone in silence.

1) Imagine yourself following Mary Magdalene as she runs to the tomb. Experience with her the shock of seeing the stone removed from the tomb. What are your feelings?

2) Run with Mary to Peter and the Beloved Disciple. Hear her voice as she tells them what has happened. Is it a voice of fear or joy?

3) Run now with the disciples to the tomb. Stay with the Beloved Disciple as he looks into the tomb. Does he go in?

4) Accompany Peter now as he goes in. What is he saying? What is his facial expression?

5) Now the disciple whom Jesus loved enters. What is his facial expression? How does his reaction differ from Peter's?

6) Spend some time talking with the risen Lord and ask him for belief like that of the Beloved Disciple.

Exploring

Mary came to the tomb while it was still dark—certainly the devotion of one who loved Jesus very much. Upon finding the stone rolled away from the tomb, she reports to the disciples her thoughts that someone had robbed the grave: "They have taken the Lord out of the tomb, and we do not know where they have laid him" (20:2). Three times Mary will emphasize this conviction. Grave robbery was not uncommon, evidenced by the fact that Emperor Claudius (A.D. 41-54) issued a decree that imposed capital punishment on anyone caught robbing a grave or destroying tombs.

The Beloved Disciple, the one who is closest to Jesus in this Gospel and who followed him all the way to the cross, continues in his role as the paradigm for all followers of Jesus. He is the first to arrive at the tomb, the first to see the burial cloths, and the first to believe immediately without seeing Jesus. Nothing at all is said about Peter's belief or disbelief; the evangelist simply tells us that Peter saw the burial cloths.

Discovering

Read John 20:11-18.

What details about Mary Magdalene do you find in this passage that are distinct from Luke 24:1-12?

Exploring

Only John gives us the detailed account of Jesus' appearance to Mary after the two disciples left the tomb. The two angels in the tomb inquire about Mary's tears. The reason is clear: "They have taken away my Lord, and I do not know where they have laid him" (20:13).

The Beloved Disciple was indeed the first to believe, but it is to Mary Magdalene that Jesus appears first. Notice the time Jesus takes with Mary. The Word of God who came down from the Father and who is one with the Father "becomes small," words frequently used by the Church Fathers to express Jesus' lowliness.

Jesus seems to adapt himself, as it were, to Mary's grief, and he lets her pour it out: "Woman, why are you weeping?" (20:15). Thinking he is a gardener, Mary does not recognize him. Jesus doesn't immediately reveal himself to this friend who loves him so much. Mary states again that the body of Jesus has been taken from the tomb, and she doesn't know where it is. "Sir, if you have carried him away, tell me where you have laid him, and I will take him away" (20:15). Only love could motivate a woman to think nothing of carrying a dead body all alone through the streets of Jerusalem. "Mary!" Without doubt, this is the voice of the good shepherd who calls his sheep by name. Mary does indeed know the voice of her Lord. She responds with "Rabbouni," perhaps a loving, pet-title for her beloved friend and teacher.

Jesus does not allow Mary to cling to him, to hold onto his earthly presence. "I am ascending to my Father and your Father, to my God and your God" (20:17). Thus Jesus seals forever by his death, resurrection and ascension his intimate relationship with her as her brother and friend.

Mary goes forth and is the first to proclaim what later in the Church was to become the criterion for apostleship: "I have seen the Lord" (20:18).

Discovering

Read John 20:19-29.

How would you describe Thomas's lack of faith in light of the role of faith in this Gospel?

Exploring

The evening of the first day of the week finds the disciples locked behind closed doors because of their fear of Jesus' enemies. Jesus enters in his resurrected body, uninhibited by locks and doors. "Peace be with you" (20:19), Jesus greets them, and he shows them his hands and feet. Then just as Yahweh had breathed life into the nostrils of the human in the beginning of creation, so now Jesus breathes spiritual life into his followers. From one who bears the scars of the cross, the wounds of Jesus' identity, they receive the Holy Spirit and the power to forgive sins. Jesus commissions them to carry on his mission, for now the Father sends them just as he sent Jesus (20:20-23). This scene seems to be John's version of Pentecost.

Thomas, however, was not present when Jesus visited with his disciples the first time. When the others proclaimed the good news, "We have seen the Lord" (20:25), Thomas refused to believe unless he could poke his finger into the hand-wounds and place his hand in the side-wound. Thomas wants physical proof, a proof that is foolproof. He illustrates for the reader the one of whom Jesus spoke in John 4:48, "Unless you can see signs and wonders you will not believe." Moreover, Thomas had been given two testimonies. First, at the Last Supper when Jesus stated that in knowing and seeing him, Thomas knows and sees the Father (14:7). Second, the disciples had already told him of Jesus' visit.

Thomas is then brought to belief by another appearance of Jesus. His confession, "My Lord and my God!" (20:28), combines both the revelation at the Last Supper that Jesus is God and the news received from the disciples that he is Lord over death and sin. The use of irony comes into play again—the disciple who doubted the witnesses utters the deepest of insights about Jesus. Jesus affirms Thomas's belief, but he also points out the blessedness of believing without seeing, something that the post-Ascension Church would need to do.

Looking Back

On Journey 15 you made the following discoveries:

- In the resurrection narratives, the Beloved Disciple carries through on his role as the paradigm for all future followers of Jesus.
- The Beloved Disciple believed without seeing the risen Lord. This kind of faith would be necessary after the Ascension.
- Jesus appeared to Mary Magdalene even before he appeared to his disciples.
- The coming of the Holy Spirit in this Gospel takes place on the first day of the week after Jesus' resurrection.

Exploring Further

Brown, Raymond E. *The Risen Christ at Eastertime*. Collegeville, Minn.: The Liturgical Press, 1991.

Martini, Carlo M. *Through Moses to Jesus: The Way of the Paschal Mystery*. Notre Dame, Ind.: Ave Maria Press, 1988.

Journey 16

An Epilogue: Jesus' Appearances in Galilee

John ended chapter 20 by giving the purpose for which this Gospel was written—"...that you may come to believe that Jesus is the Messiah, the Son of God, and that through believing you may have life in his name" (20:31). One would think that with this statement, John had given this Gospel a proper ending, but there is one more chapter that tells of Jesus' appearances in Galilee.

Chapter 21 is often referred to as the "epilogue": something that was added onto the Gospel at a later period, but before it was accepted as one of the books declared normative for Christian living. The style of written expression is different from the rest of the Gospel, but the fact that it carries through with some of the same Johannine themes leads many scholars to believe that it was written by a member of the same Johannine community.

Discovering

Read John 21:1-14.

Where does this incident occur?

What practical things does Jesus do for his disciples in this passage?

Exploring

Besides this encounter of Jesus with his disciples, one other incident in the Fourth Gospel took place at the Sea of Tiberias in Galilee—the feeding of the five thousand in John 6. On both occasions, Jesus gave those present bread and fish, and in both events, Jesus is the host. The first incident took place during Jesus' ministry on earth; the second occurred after his resurrection. Therefore, it seems probable that the writer was addressing Christians who needed to realize that Jesus continues to provide for his followers in his risen life as he did during his earthly life. His caring relationship with those who believe in him—a relationship that was expressed in the allegory of the good shepherd, his washing the feet of his disciples and all his mighty and compassionate deeds—would not cease with the absence of his physical presence.

The catch of fish is also connected with the feeding of the five thousand by use of the word "draw" (*helkyein* in Greek). Attention to the translation of the Greek is important for understanding the connection. In 21:6, the disciples were unable to "draw" (*helkyein*) the net because it was so heavy with fish. In 6:44, Jesus stated that faith or coming to Jesus is the result of being "drawn" (*helkyein*) by the Father. In 12:32, Jesus promised that when he was lifted up in his exaltation to the Father through the cross, he would "draw" (*helkyein*) all people to himself. The story of the catch of fish, then, shows us that the risen Jesus will continue to "draw" people to himself through the work of his followers. But they cannot draw people to the risen Lord on their own strength, just as the disciples could not catch any fish without the help of Jesus. Following the commands of Jesus, however, they were able to draw in a great number of fish. Many scholars think that the net is a symbol of the Church. Fishing for disciples was a theme in Luke's Gospel; for example, Jesus told the disciples after the big catch that they would be catching people for the Kingdom (Luke 5:1-11).

If Saint Jerome is correct that according to Greek zoologists, there existed only 153 kinds of fish, then the significance of the 153 fish in this passage may mean that Jesus is telling his followers to bring people of all nations to belief in him. This interpretation would fit with the tradition in Matthew 28:19 to make disciples of all nations.

Discovering

Read John 21:15-24.

How many times does Jesus ask Peter if he loves him? Does that correspond with anything else related to Peter?

Exploring

John 21:15-24 deals specifically with the roles of Peter and the Beloved Disciple. In the first passage that we examined in this journey, Peter had a leadership role. At the command of Jesus, he was the one who went out and "drew" the net full of fish onto the shore. His role is not independent of Jesus.

Jesus reaffirms Peter's leadership position as caretaker of the flock when, in a threefold commission, he tells him to "feed my lambs," "tend my sheep" and "feed my sheep" (21:15-17). Thus the sheep and lambs belong to Jesus. Peter is to carry on the work of the good shepherd, and like the good shepherd, he, too, will lay down his life on a cross (21:18-19). The threefold inquiry about Peter's love for him corresponds to Peter's threefold denial of Jesus in the passion narrative.

Discovering

Reread John 21:1-14.

What is John's role in the passage?

Exploring

One of the themes in this Gospel is that of witness to Jesus. We have seen that John the Baptist (1:19-34), Andrew and Philip (1:35-51), the Samaritan woman (4:1-42) and the man born blind (9:1-41) all bore testimony to Jesus. Jesus himself bore testimony to the Father and to his identity as one with the Father and the one sent by him.

Now in John 21:7, the disciple whom Jesus loved gives testimony by his statement to Peter, "It is the Lord!" The identification of Jesus as Lord was an early form of creed used by the Christians. "Lord" identified Jesus as the "Lord" of the second creation story (Genesis 2:4b—3:24) who initiated the first creation. Jesus began a new creation in which sin and death no longer held dominion over humanity. The title "Lord" also emphasized the intimacy of God among us in Jesus. Just as the Lord had a personal relationship with Adam and Eve (he walked and talked with them in the garden), so even more so is God present in an intimate relationship with us in Jesus, the Lord.

Therefore, the Beloved Disciple's proclamation to Peter, "It is the Lord!" highlights his role as witness, and therefore stands as the paradigm for all future disciples. As chapter 21 indicates, the Beloved Disciple will continue to witness: Even after his death, his witness would continue in the Gospel.

Discovering

Now that you have finished the journeys in this book, take about forty minutes to do the following exercise:

- Sit alone with your eyes closed and breath deeply and slowly to become relaxed.
- Begin by thinking of Jesus as you found him to be in this Gospel. Perhaps as the good shepherd, the one whom the Father sent from himself and so on.
- Spend some time being grateful to Jesus for all you have learned in this study. Be specific in naming some of the insights you received that seem to bring you into a closer relationship with him.
- Ask Jesus how you might nourish the graces you received in this study. Let him speak in the silence of your heart.

Looking Back

On Journey 16 you made the following discoveries:

- The Fourth Gospel's first ending in 20:20-31 reminds us that the importance of belief in Jesus as the messiah and Son of God motivated the evangelist to write this Gospel.

- Chapter 21 may have been added some time after the first twenty chapters to understand the leadership role of Peter in the Church as well as the role of the Beloved Disciple (model for all followers) as witness to Jesus through his words in the Church.
- The title "Lord," proclaimed by the Beloved Disciple, indicates both the divinity of Jesus as well as God's intimate relationship with us.

Exploring Further

Minear, Paul. *John: The Martyr's Gospel*. New York: Pilgrim Press, 1984.

Grassi, Joseph A. *The Secret Identity of the Beloved Disciple*. Mahwah, N.J.: Paulist Press, 1992.

Annotated Bibliography

Brown, Raymond E. *The Death of the Messiah*. 2 vols. New York: Doubleday, 1994.

These two volumes provide an extensive commentary on the passion narratives of all four Gospels. They contain 1,608 pages that offer information concerning every aspect of the passion narratives. Though a scholarly work, it is accessible to all.

_____. *The Gospel According to John (I-XII; XIII-XXI)*. Anchor Bible Series. Garden City, N.Y.: Doubleday, 1989, 1970.

Even though this two-volume commentary is old, as books go today, it still is a valuable and very comprehensive resource. Important words or phrases that lose their richness when translated from Greek into English are explained so as to make the Gospel more understandable. There is a thorough introduction to the Gospel, a commentary after each passage and a good appendix of the study of important Greek words in the Gospel.

_____. *The Gospel and Epistles of John*, 4th ed. Collegeville, Minn.: The Liturgical Press, 1988.

A concise commentary written especially for people who do not have a scholarly background in Scripture. It carries the text of the Gospel at the top of the page with the commentary on the text at the lower half of the page. It has a lectionary plus review questions for each chapter at the end of the book. Father Brown is one of the world's most renowned New Testament scholars and is highly respected by both the Church and the academic world.

_____. *New Testament Essays*. Garden City, N.Y.: Image Books, 1965.

Among these essays on the New Testament, Father Brown presents "The Theology and Background of the Fourth Gospel" and "The Relation Between the Fourth Gospel and the Synoptic Gospels"—essays that are very helpful in understanding the Gospel of John.

_____. *The Risen Christ at Eastertime*. Collegeville, Minn.: The Liturgical Press, 1991.

Father Brown interprets the resurrection narratives in the four Gospels. Chapters 4 and 5 are devoted to the resurrection in the Fourth Gospel. It is a clearly presented treatise, easily understood by those who do not have a scholarly background in Scripture.

Brown, Raymond E., Karl Dunfried, Jospeh Fitzmyer and John Rheumann, editors. *Mary in the New Testament*. Mahwah, N.J.: Paulist Press, 1978.

This book is the fruit of collaborative study by both Roman Catholic and Protestant scholars. Chapter 7 is specifically devoted to the Mother of Jesus in the Gospel of John. Simply and clearly presented, both the scholar and the nonprofessional person, especially those interested in Marian issues involved in ecumenical dialogue, will find this book both helpful and interesting.

Collins, Raymond F. *John and His Witness*. Zacchaeus Studies: New Testament. Collegeville, Minn.: Michael Glazier/The Liturgical Press, 1991.

Collins provides a study of the characters who make their appearance in the first chapter of John's Gospel. Beginning with John the Baptist, he continues with those who are brought to Jesus: the unnamed disciple, Peter, Andrew, Philip and Nathanael. According to Collins, each has a role to play in the Gospel as well as in the formation of the Johannine community. An interesting and clearly written book for the professional biblical scholar and for the nonprofessional as well.

Comblin, Jose, trans. Carl Kabut. *Sent From the Father. Meditations on the Fourth Gospel*. Maryknoll, N.Y.: Orbis Books, 1979.

The Gospel of John is shown to focus on the person of Jesus and his impact on others. The book is easy to read and calls the reader to a spirituality based on mission.

Countryman, William. *The Mystical Way in the Fourth Gospel: Crossing Over Into God*. Revised edition. Valley Forge, Pa.: Trinity Press, 1994.

Countryman maintains that John is guiding his readers toward conversion through Christian initiation to mystical union with the person of Jesus Christ.

Eller, Vernard. *The Beloved Disciple: His Name, His Story, His Thought*. Grand Rapids, Mich.: Wm. B. Eerdmans Publishing Co., 1987.

Eller takes a Sherlock Holmes approach in his efforts to identify the Beloved Disciple in the Fourth Gospel. He steers away from academic scholarship to provide the lay reader with an intriguing yet serious search of the identity of the unknown disciple.

Grassi, Joseph A. *The Secret Identity of the Beloved Disciple*. Mahwah, N.J.: Paulist Press, 1992.

In a meticulous effort to build a character sketch of the creative mind behind the Fourth Gospel, Grassi investigates the identity of the Beloved Disciple. He concludes that the one whom Jesus loved was "adopted" by Jesus as a lad, and that the ties between them aroused jealousy among the disciples. The book's greatest asset is the study of the Beloved Disciple as developed in the Gospel.

Heil, John P. *Blood and Water. The Death and Resurrection of Jesus in John 18-21*. Catholic Biblical Quarterly Monograph Series 27. Washington, D.C.: The Catholic Biblical Association of America, 1995.

Heil's interpretation employs narrative criticism and is directed more to persons with a professional biblical background, although it is possible for the non-scholar to understand since most of the Greek words are translated. Anyone in the field of literature may find the narrative approach helpful and intriguing.

Hengel, Martin. *Crucifixion*. Translated by John Bowden. Philadelphia: Fortress Press, 1977.

Hengel, a German biblical scholar, gives us a general exposition of the widespread employment of the cruel practice of crucifixion in the Roman empire, particularly in Roman-occupied Palestine in the first century. His conclusions demonstrate for the reader the offensiveness of the cross in the Christian message: that Jesus—redeemer, Lord and God—underwent the most contemptible abasement that could be imagined. The facts are well documented and clearly presented.

Karris, Robert J. *Jesus and the Marginalized in John's Gospel*. Zacchaeus Studies: New Testament. Collegeville, Minn.: Michael Glazier/The Liturgical Press, 1990.

A concise and readable little volume, this intriguing work provides a rare look at the rich and the poor in John's Gospel, a topic rarely treated from this perspective. What is so obvious in the Synoptic Gospels, biblical scholar Father Karris has ferreted out and presented for further thought and study in the Fourth Gospel: that the Messiah who ministered to the marginalized also became marginalized himself. A real treat in brief form!

Koester, Craig R. *Symbolism in the Fourth Gospel. Meaning, Mystery, Community*. Minneapolis: Fortress Press, 1995.

Koester's treatment of the symbols in the Fourth Gospel provides an excellent key to understanding the Gospel. This book casts light upon such symbols as light and darkness, bread, living water and other images of important theological content. He argues that Johannine symbolism would have been accessible to a wide spectrum of readers; it would have fostered in the Christian a sense of identity that was distinct from the world, while motivating the reader to missionary engagement with the world. Both student and scholar will find unequaled value in this volume.

Kysar, Robert. *John, the Maverick Gospel*. Atlanta: John Knox, 1976.

Kysar gives us a clear, simple introduction to the theology, concepts and vocabulary of the Fourth Gospel. This book is an excellent resource for adults to get a better understanding of the Gospel of John.

La Potterie, Ignace de. *The Hour of Jesus*. New York: Alba House, 1983.

This distinguished Belgian priest and biblical scholar furnishes us with a simple and straightforward analysis of the passion and resurrection of Jesus in the Fourth Gospel following the methods of modern interpretation. True to the theology of this Gospel, La Potterie presents the passion of Jesus as the elevation and triumph of Christ that culminates in the resurrection.

Martini, S.J., Carlo M. *Through Moses to Jesus. The Way of the Paschal Mystery*. Notre Dame, Ind.: Ave Maria Press, 1988.

In a simple, straightforward, pastoral style, Martini provides an excellent example of reflecting on Scripture in one's spiritual life. He sets forth the similarities between Moses and Jesus, for example, how both hold God's will to be paramount in their lives, and how both learned patience, acceptance and service.

Minear, Paul. *John: The Martyr's Gospel*. New York: Pilgrim Press, 1984.

The word "martyr" in this book's title has to do with its Greek meaning, "to witness." Minear, in a clear and simple way, emphasizes Jesus' role as witness whose witness is in turn to be imitated by his disciples. This book is especially helpful for interpreting John 12—21.

Petersen, Norman R. *The Gospel of John and the Sociology of Light: Language and Characterization in the Fourth Gospel*. Valley Forge, Pa.: Trinity Press International, 1993.

This sociological study of light purports that the language used in this Gospel was ordinary language used in a way to make it oppositional in character, and therefore it functioned socially to distinguish the Johannine believers from their opponents. This book is aimed at the more professional person in the biblical field. However, though Petersen deals with many Greek words, they are almost always translated for the reader, and if interested, almost anyone could glean much from it.

Rensberger, David. *Johannine Faith and Liberating Community*. Philadelphia: Westminster Press, 1988.

Rensberger maintains that the Johannine community was itself an alternative society, a counterculture which lived the message of the Messiah. He relates various aspects of the Fourth Gospel to liberation theology and to contemporary questions about the role of the Church in the world. An interesting book, clearly presented, and well worth reading.

Senior, Donald. *The Passion of Jesus in the Gospel of John*. Passion Series. Collegeville, Minn.: Michael Glazier/The Liturgical Press, 1991.

Father Senior notes that "this Gospel manages to state its entire message in practically every passage of the Gospel" (15). Hence, his commentary on the passion and death of Jesus in John's Gospel begins with an explanation of key themes that lead the reader through the Gospel of John to the passion. The small volume is reflective of Father Senior's scholarship presented on a popular level.

Servotte, Herman. *According to John*. London: Darton, Longman, & Todd, 1992/94.

This small book provides a literary reading of the Fourth Gospel. Father Servotte (an English professor) focuses on the text as a literary writing. His method highlights important theological questions and accentuates things about the human condition that are generally missed in the ordinary commentaries. It is a book that will stimulate the imagination and provide a sound basis for one's life of faith.

Stanley, David. *Jesus in Gethsemani*. New York: Paulist Press, 1980.

In this book, Stanley sets forth a study of the Gethsemani narrative in all four Gospels. He opens the book with a discussion of the significance for Christian living that the contemplation of Jesus' earthly life provides. The last part is devoted to John's creative reinterpretation of Jesus' final prayer before his passion, death and resurrection.

Thompson, Marianne Meye. *The Incarnate Word: Perspectives on Jesus in the Fourth Gospel*. Peabody, Mass.: Hendrickson, 1988.

Thompson gives us a study that is especially helpful in understanding Johannine Christology and the role of the signs in the Gospel of John. Though simply written and accessible to the layperson, this book is based on good scholarship.

Yee, Gale A. *Jewish Feasts and the Gospel of John*. Zacchaeus Studies. Collegeville, Minn.: Michael Glazier/The Liturgical Press, 1988.

Yee focuses on the major feasts that occur in the Gospel of John (Sabbath, Passover, Tabernacles, and Dedication), and how their understanding is crucial for comprehending the message of this Gospel. The book is good scholarship made accessible to the ordinary reader who does not have a scholarly background.